An Inspiring Journey

By
DARSHAN SINGH SARAI, Ph.D.

*To the memory of my wife and Dar Ji,
and for our family.*

© by Darshan Singh Sarai, Ph.D.   All Rights Reserved

No part of this book may be reproduced, photocopied or utilized by any storage device or retrieval system without the express written permission of the author. Information contained herein may be used by educational institutions where appropriate to further the awareness of Indian culture and Sikh philosophy.

The events, recollections and relationships described herein are told from Darshan Singh Sarai's point of view. As such, they reflect his personal remembrance.

Life Stories Imprint
A Division of Magic Mountain Press
ISBN# 978-0-9715946-2-3

Library of Congress Control Number: 2017908202
First Edition, June 2017

Sarai, Darshan Singh: (b) 1932 -

Other Titles:
Faith and the Journey
  Published 2010 by Magic Mountain Press
Water Treatment Made Simple for Operators
  Published 2005 by John Wiley and Sons
Basic Chemistry for Water and Wastewater Operators
  Published 2002 by the American Water Works Association

Printed in the United States of America
by Lightning Source, Inc.
Published by Magic Mountain Press
P.O. Box 1933
Asheville, NC 28802

Front Cover Photo: Mohinder at Sri Harmandir Sahib
Back Cover Photo: Front of Mohinder's Hoshiarpur home

Acknowledgment

I sincerely acknowledge the help of my daughters, Sumandeep, Bina and Nina, particularly Bina being at home and with an excellent memory of lots of events, for their continuous and encouraging support throughout this project; Bhen Ji and Mohan auntie for helping me with information about Mohinder's childhood; Mohinder's brothers and sisters, especially Arvinderpal Singh, President/ Owner of Digital Printing Services, Kansas City for providing the valuable information, suggestions and pictures about Mohinder's life before her marriage and an excellent job of printing services; our grandchildren, especially Esha for reading and editing the first draft and many helpful suggestions to improve it; Karon Korp, President of Magic Mountain Press for valuable suggestions and publishing the book; and all others who directly and indirectly helped me to complete this work.

Preface

When I was writing my life story, *Faith and the Journey*, my wife, Mohinderjit Kaur Sudha-Sarai, showed some interest about her life story. I said, "Mohinder it is a great idea for our children and future generations to know about their roots. God willing I would love to do it." It was a great idea as her background was quite different than mine. She came from an affluent urban family whereas I came from a small village and a farming family. We had such a wonderful married life. A friend of ours once commented, "Yours's is a love marriage. I replied no; it is a marriage love." Our love developed after marriage through mutual respect by caring and sharing while living together.

We tried to keep our children in touch with both sides, maternal and paternal, of the family by visiting them in India. They enjoyed staying in both homes and by walking the same streets which we both did in our childhood. In 1996, Sumandeep planned and had the second birthday party of her son, Ben, in Hoshiarpur home in Mohinder's bed room where Sumandeep was born in 1960. It was a fun party with cake baked by Mohinder's mother/ Bhen Ji, and other food and party decorations from our favorite shops. The party was attended by Sumandeep, her husband, Mark; Nina, her husband, Sukhdev, her daughter, Karuna; and members of Mohinder's side of the family.

Our daughters and three grandchildren visited and lived in Jande Sarai (my native village) home in 2006 and had Bina's 40th birthday party there. Esha, our granddaughter, visited both homes in 2014 for a short time, and then in 2017 for a longer period. We always felt that both sides of the family were one extended large family. Members of the large family enjoy being together at special occasions like festivals, birthdays and marriages, etc. There is a lot of mutual respect and helping attitude among them. We are blessed and thankful to God for such a caring family.

Mohinder was an exceptional and inspirational person for the whole family. She touched the lives of all the members of the family and earned their love and respect. As far as I am concerned, I consider myself one of the luckiest persons in the world to have had Mohinder as my wife and mother of our three wonderful children. She gave us precious life values, hopefully those would be the guidelines to live happy and fulfilled lives for generations to come. She was an exemplary Sikh living a realistic and practical Sikh way of life. She tried to enjoy every moment of life. This work is a humble attempt to describe Mohinder's life. I hope that this attempt has achieved that goal and put some of those memories in words for posterity.

Contents

1. Introduction 1
2. Childhood 3
3. College Education 25
4. Mohinder, the Artist 31
5. Wedding and Married Life 41
6. University of Alberta 61
7. Kelowna BC 83
8. Mountain Grove USA 97
9. Neosho, Missouri 107
10. Kansas City 121
11. Retired Life 133
12. Mohinder, Traveler 145
13. Mohinder and Esha's College Education 239
14. Mohinder's 75th Birthday 247
15. Exemplary Person 255

Chapter 1
INTRODUCTION

GOD has blessed us all with the gift of life and to each of us a different life journey. Each one of us is provided with basic and essential resources such as family, a mind and body to succeed in life, both materially and spiritually. Then, it is up to an individual to use them to achieve whatever goal that person pursues.

The beauty of the gift of life is that each one of us is granted just a certain amount, unknown to us, of time (life span) to achieve our goals. Therefore, time is the most precious and uncertain resource, and we need to use every moment of it, wisely, by doing the best we can. The ultimate goal of life, according to Sikh philosophy, is to be one with God and have no more reincarnations. It is achieved by our deeds such as service of humanity performed with humility, earning our living honestly, sharing with others and meditating on the name of God. Our deeds are judged in the court of God after we depart this world.

Mohinder was a very realistic and practical person who made the best of life and enjoyed every moment of it to the fullest. She often quoted the Sri Guru Granth Sahib Ji (Sikh Holy Scripture) *"Jaa too marai val hai taa ki-aa muhchhadaa. Tudh sabh kichh maino saupiaa jaa tayraa bandaa.* Meaning, when you are on my side, God, then I don't need anyone else's help. You have blessed me with everything as I am your devoted servant." She practiced religion in the real sense, made it part of her life, and became an example for the family.

She had so many great qualities and accomplishments: She was a gifted artist who painted beautiful (some award winning) paintings in her college years and later, a teacher who taught preschool for 20 years with awards for her work with children. She was a devoted tennis player, an exciting vacationer and traveler, a highly supportive and understanding wife and a compassionate and caring mother and grandmother with three loving daughters and seven grandchildren. She was a talented cook and a cheerful host who enjoyed receiving visiting relatives and friends. She cheerfully shared her resources with others. She enjoyed giving whenever and wherever it was needed. She often said that God has blessed us - let us share with those who are in need. She was a responsible team player in the Sarai Family Team and a guiding light for the family.

Chapter 2
FAMILY AND CHILDHOOD

Most of the information about Mohinder's childhood is either from Mohinder herself or from her family members - in particular, her father Sardar (S. for short) Narinder Singh Ji. Sardar, means a leader and is used before the name of an adult male turbaned Sikh. I had the opportunity to spend enough time with him to benefit from his wisdom and learn about their family.

Mohinder was born on May 14, 1939 in Amritsar, the holiest city of Sikhs, to father S. Narinder Singh Ji and mother Bibi Kartar Kaur Ji. Respectfully and affectionately they were addressed as Dar Ji and Bi Ji. Both her paternal and maternal families were affluent and well-known in the region and were exemplary humble people who practiced Sikhism in the real sense in every walk of life.

Amritsar

The city of Amritsar was historically known as Ram Das Pura named after its founder, Sri Guru Ram Das Sahib (the fourth Sikh Guru). He bought the land from the owner of the village Tung in 1573. Plans were drawn by Sri Guru Amar Das Sahib (the third Sikh Guru) and passed on to Sri Guru Ram Das Sahib. The city's name was changed to Amritsar after the sacred Sarover (tank), Amritsar, meaning the tank of immortal water. Sri Guru Ram Das Ji began building the Sarover in 1574 and it was completed three years later. There is a continuous flow of water through the Sarover. Water comes from the canal, Upper Bari Doab, of the river Ravi.

Sri Guru Arjan Dev Sahib (the fifth Sikh Guru) designed the building, Sri Harmandir Sahib, the God's

Temple, to be built in the center of the Sarover. The foundation stone was laid in Dec. 1588 by a Muslim Sufi Saint, Pir Mian Mir Ji, a friend of Sri Guru Arjan Dev Sahib. The Sri Harmandir Sahib building was completed in 1601. It has four doors, in four directions to show that the temple is open to all humanity. It is estimated a daily average of 100,000 people visit the holy shrine to bathe in the Sarover, worship, and have their wishes granted. They also partake in the free meal (Langar), a hallmark of Sikh Gurdwaras (Sikh temples). The present day Sri Harmandir Sahib was serviced in 1830 by Maharaja Ranjit Singh by getting the outside of second floor covered with gold plating, which gives the distinct golden look and thus the name the Golden Temple. Maharaja Ranjit Singh was a devoted Sikh ruler, who ruled Panjab/Punjab from 1799-1839. Panjab means land of "five rivers". The name comes from the word Panj- ab, which stands for five waters.

The holy Sarover is 500ft. square with a 65 ft. square platform and a 40 ft. square Sri Harmandir Sahib building, the Sanctum Santorum, in its center. The Sri Guru Granth Sahib (Sikh Scripture), the seat of God, was installed in 1604. There has been continuous Gurbani Kirtan (recital of hymns from Sri Guru Granth Sahib) at the Sri Harmandir Sahib from Sri Guru Arjan Dev Sahib's time to the present day. Sri Harmandir Sahib is connected to the perimeter of the Sarover by a 200ft long bridge. At the other end of bridge is the Darshni Deori which leads to a marble Parkarmia (circumambulatory) which goes around the Sarover. In front of Darshni Deori is Sri Akal Takhat Sahib (throne of the timeless God). It was built in 1608 by Sri Guru Hargovind Sahib (sixth Sikh Guru) with the help of Baba Budha Ji and Bhai Gurdas Ji. Sri Guru Hargovind Sahib used to hold his court here to make temporal decisions, in a spiritual way, for Sikhs.

In Parkarmia there are three Ber Trees (Indian jujube): Dukhbhanjani Ber, Baba Budha Ji's Ber and Lachi Ber all of great historical importance. Dukhbhanjani Ber, perhaps the oldest, is on the southeast side where there is ladies' and men's bathrooms. Historically it is known as a place for curing bodily diseases, as once a leper was cured by having a bath in a nearby pool. Baba Budha Ji's Ber is on the northeast side. Baba Budha Ji used to sit under this and supervise the construction of Sarover and Sri Harmandir Sahib. Lachi Ber is on the right side of the Darshni Deori under which Sri Guru Arjan Dev Sahib used to sit to supervise the construction of Sri Harmandir Sahib. All three Bers are more than 400 years old. A visit to Sri Harmandir Sahib gives a person a uniquely mystical and spiritual feeling. A couplet from Sri Guru Granth Sahib ji describes it as, ***"Dithae Sabhae Thaav Nahi Tudh Jeha"***, meaning 'one saw various places but none of them is like you.'

Amritsar grew to a city with merchants from all over who established their businesses. It had business bazars all around Sri Harmandir sahib as well as housing. It became the spiritual, cultural, educational and business center of Panjab. Present day Amritsar's population is over 1.1 million people.

Sri Harmandir Sahib Ji

Amritsar is only about 17 miles east of the Pakistan border and 31 miles from Lahore, Pakistan.

Family

Dar Ji's father was S. Gurdit Singh, son of Mahtab Singh son of Prem Singh son of Chaudhry Karam Singh. Chaudhry is a title given to a leader of a group of people. A Street in the city of Amritsar is named after Chaudhry Karam Singh as Koocha Chaudhry Karam Singh which is between Chowk (crossing) Baba Attal and Chawk Karoorii Mal. Dar Ji showed us his ancestral home and a small playground where he used to play with his cousins. The family participated in daily services at Sri Harmandir Sahib, Golden Temple, which is only a few blocks away from Dar Ji's ancestral home. Dar Ji's father serviced a window pane next to the stairs on the North East side of the second floor of Sri Harmandir Sahib, in memory of his late wife.

Mohinder's Dada Ji, S. Gurdit Singh Ji

Dar Ji's dad was a structural engineer who later settled in Lyallpur, a progressive industrial city, also known as Faisalabad (in modern-day Pakistan) which is about 100 miles west of Amritsar. He worked as an estimator for buildings. Dar Ji was born in Lyallpur on Feb 2, 1913, where he grew up and was educated as a civil engineer. He was the oldest son. His mother, Bibi Bhagwan Kaur, passed on when he was about 6 months old. He was raised by two of his elder sisters as well as his step-mother, who had three children of her own: Two sons and a daughter named

Harbhajan Singh, Pritpal Singh and Kuldeep Kaur. I had a chance to meet them all. Dar Ji's sisters, Sant Kaur and Kuldeep Kaur were living in Amritsar when we lived there years later. Mohinder and I enjoyed their company and hospitality on many occasions.

Dar Ji shared some of his childhood stories with me. I remember two of those quite vividly: Playing "hooky" at the Lyallpur city Clock Tower located in the center of the city, and one of a wrestler who considered Dar Ji his guru, determined through a math test.

He told me that when he started elementary school, he did not like the school; however, his dad insisted that he attend. He would get ready for school with a packed lunch, leave home and come back at the normal school closing time. His dad asked the teacher about Dar Ji's performance in class and came to know that Dar ji was not attending the school. One day Dar Ji's dad followed him and caught him playing with his friends at the clock tower. After that he became a good student and had good grades, especially in math.

Clock Tower, Lyallpur

Once a well-known wrestler from Lyallpur visited Dar Ji's school to find a young "guru". He was told by some wise person to find a young guru through a math test to seek his blessing to have a successful wrestling career. The wrestler gave the test to Dar Ji's class. Dar ji solved the problem and the wrestler touched his feet and thus found a guru. The wrestler would carry Dar Ji on his shoulders to his matches, touch his feet and ask his blessings before starting the match. The wrestler won most of his matches.

Bi Ji's family had successful businesses in several cities besides Amritsar (Hoshiarpur and Nankana Sahib, now in Pakistan, to mention a few) with headquarters and principal residence (10 Daswanda Singh Rd.) in Amritsar. Nankana Sahib, the birthplace of Guru Nanak Dev Ji is one of the holiest places of Sikhs. Guru Nanak Dev Ji is the founder of Sikhism. Bi Ji's dad, S. Ishar Singh Arora, respectfully and affectionately called Bha ji by the family, was one of the richest people in Amritsar, perhaps in Panjab. In Amritsar, a road, Hukam Singh Rd., is named after his cousin S. Hukam Singh. The road runs North-South between Company Bagh and Shivala Colony. It is quite close to the family's home. It is a matter of pride for the family. Mohinder often talked about it.

Mohinder's Nana Ji, S. Ishar Singh Arora

Bi Ji's mother, Bibi Harnam Kaur addressed as *Jhaaiee Ji* by the family also came from a rich business family dealing mainly in jewelry. Bi ji was the oldest of the seven siblings, four sisters and three bothers. Sisters, Balbir Kaur, Avtar Kaur, and Manmohan Kaur and brothers,

Bhagwant Singh, Jagjit Singh and Avtar Singh. Bi Ji's family was also very religious, serving at Sri Harmandir

Sahib and Nankana Sahib Gurdwaras (Sikh Temples) in several capacities.

Jhaaiee Ji, Mata Harnam Kaur

Dar ji and Bi Ji got married in 1934 at the ages of 21 and 18 years respectively. They started their married life in Lyallpur. They soon built their own home in a suburb. Dar Ji was working for the Panjab Government in Lahore, the Capital of Panjab province under British rule. Shockingly, Dar Ji's dad had a severe heart attack and passed on in 1937 at the age of 48. Dar Ji was informed by a telegram while at work in Lahore. He told me that it was the saddest day in his life. He was so heartbroken that he did not want to live at Lyallpur anymore and moved back to Amritsar.

Dar Ji, S. Narinder Singh

In Amritsar he was employed as a civil engineer in the Panjab Canal Department. He had three daughters, Jagdish, Mohinder and Malvinder. Jagdish was about 3 years older than Mohinder. She died at the age of about 3 years in a fire accident. It was another tragedy for the family. Malvinder is two years younger than Mohinder. Dar ji told me a scary incident about Mohinder's childhood. When she was a toddler she was given a bath in a small tank by her uncle Pritpal Singh (Dar Ji's youngest brother). He left the water running and forgot her, to answer someone's call. She had almost drowned when someone noticed and got her out. She was unconscious and not breathing. The family panicked and thought that she died. She was put on a large pot face down and revived by patting her back. She threw up the water and started breathing. In the meantime, someone had called Dar Ji at work and informed him that Mohinder had drowned. Dar Ji was shocked and crying. He immediately left the office and came home. Instead of grieving and sadness there was a great celebration by distributing sweets and money. To his amazement, Dar Ji found Mohinder well and alive. Dar Ji said that he was so happy and thankful to God to see Mohinder. Mohinder was so loved and important that her Nana Ji said that Mohinder had saved two more lives, her mother's and her grandmother's by surviving. Whenever Mohinder's drowning story came up, I said to Mohinder, "God has saved us both for each other." Like Mohinder, I almost died in a bonfire after getting severely burned when I was a little baby.

India was going through political turmoil, in 1940s, due to the Indian Freedom Movement against British Rule and Amritsar was one of the hot spots and very active in that movement. Considering the situation, Dar Ji moved to Hoshiarpur as Mohinder's maternal family had already moved there and had quite an established business. Hoshiarpur was a safer place than Amritsar. Dar Ji built a nice two-story brick house in a suburban area on the west side of town on the Jullundur- Hoshiarpur Rd. next to the two-story large brick building owned by his in-laws with first floor for storage and second for residential purposes.

It is away from the city with mango groves, open fields and only a few other houses around. The area is now called Gokal Nagar. The building is a land mark with a Quote from Sri Guru Granth Sahib Ji about Sri Guru Amar Das Sahib Ji, "**Bhalae Amardas Gun Thaerae Thaeree Oupamaa Thohi Ban Aavai**" (meaning, Guru Amar Das, your glorious virtues are so sublime that your praises belong only to you), on the front wall. This building was later bought by Dar Ji; and the family moved into it. Dar Ji started a textile business named Narinder Textiles, with handlooms making various types of cloth and specializing in corduroy.

His corduroy cloth was so good and popular that Dar Ji got a contract from the big and prestigious Ashoka Hotel all the way in New Delhi for its curtains.

The rest of the Mohinder's maternal family was living in the main city in the Gaushala bazar close to their business which is about 4 miles east of Dar Ji's house. Both families were very close. Mohinder used to spend most of her time at her grandparents' house with her best friend Manmohan - Bi Ji's youngest sister, who is only 3 years older than Mohinder. Mohinder called her Mohan Auntie. They were lifelong best friends and dubbed as M and M by me. Mohinder's youngest maternal uncle, S. Avtar Singh Arora, was their close friend as well. The three of them often had fun together such as playing games like cards, carom board, going to the movies and eating out. He used to treat them. Often it was an all-evening fun time, starting with some meat snacks like chicken, shish kabab, tea or coffee and then a movie. After that they used to have a full dinner at some of the best restaurants in Hoshiarpur.

To escape the summer heat, Dar Ji often took his family to Dalhousie, a hill station in the Chamba District of Himachal Pradesh province. It is a beautiful summer resort situated in the Dhauladhar mountain range of the Himalayas, surrounded by snowcapped peaks. It is 6,000 to 9,000 ft. above sea level and is about 100 miles North of Hoshiarpur. Dar Ji told some interesting stories about his trips to this hill station and one of those is when Mohinder saved Malvinder from falling into the gorge which was very deep and dangerous. Malvinder slipped and Mohinder pulled her back thus saving her life.

Dar Ji and Bi Ji in Dalhousie

Mohinder told me a recurring childhood story, that when she would get in trouble for doing something wrong, Bi Ji would try to punish her. However, Mohinder would run around and around the bed until Bi Ji would give up trying to catch her, as she had health problems and could not run fast enough without getting short of breath. Mohinder was a beautiful baby and loved by everyone on both sides of the family, being the oldest grandchild, to the point that nobody would stay mad at her. Her uncle, Bhra ji Bhagwant Singh (Bhra Ji, meaning brother dear) Arora was a member of the Amritsar Lion's Club and sometimes he would take her to the club to show her to his friends. He called her a Japanese doll due to her being so pretty. Once Bhra Ji, at the club meeting had Mohinder with him. While enjoying the meeting and exceptional good behavior of Mohinder which was noted by the members, something happened. There was an interesting talk by the speaker and everybody was listening very attentively. All of a sudden there was a sound of ice crushing. Mohinder took an ice cube from her drink and chewed on it. Bhra Ji looked at her, the speaker paused and Mohinder realized her mistake. She felt bad and said, "Sorry". Members smiled and said it was OK baby. Mohinder learned her lesson.

Primary/Elementary School

At age 5, Mohinder started her elementary education at Government Elementary School Hoshiarpur for Girls. School was about a mile from her home in a beautiful setting surrounded by the mango groves and away from the main population.

Mohan Auntie was already attending the same school so it was quite easy for Mohinder to adjust. Mohinder had a black dot like flat mole, a birth mark, on her forehead between her eyebrows that resembled a Vindi, a makeup dot, applied by women. It got her in trouble with her teacher whenever she forgot to do her homework. The teacher would scold Mohinder by saying, "How come you never forget to apply vindi on your forehead and yet you don't remember the homework." As the teacher did not know that it was a birth mark. Mohinder was very particular about her looks. Once, Mohinder forgot to use kajal (eye liner) and Malvinder did not. Mohinder realized that she forgot the kajal while on her way to school. After reaching school she asked Malvinder to join her in the bathroom. Once there, Mohinder said, "Good sisters share things." Malvinder agreed. Mohinder said she forgot to apply kajal, and noted Malvinder had too much in her eyes. "So let me have some." Mohinder took some of the kajal from Malvinder's eyes with her finger and applied it on her eyes. She said "thank you sister" and felt good. This story became quite entertaining whenever Mohinder's makeup topic came up. Being good sisters they sometimes fought with each other like normal sisters. An interesting event was a dream, in which Mohinder said rather loudly, "Hey Malvinder, where is my pajama?" and Malvinder responded, "I don't know about your pajama. May be it is in the bathroom. You should take care of your things." Dar Ji and Bhen Ji heard that and talked about it in the morning. Mohinder and Malvinder did not have any clue about the dream.

Mohinder was in 3rd grade when India got independence from British Rule on Aug. 15, 1947. It was a great time to celebrate the freedom for which India fought for so long with indescribable sacrifices at the hands of the British Government. To mention a few: the massacre at Jullianwala Bagh in 1919, Amritsar; hanging of freedom fighters, Bhagat Singh, Rajguru, Sukhdev, Udham Singh and dying of Lala Lagpat Rai from police clubs. They are known as martyrs in Indian history. Besides that, India was divided and a new country, Pakistan, was formed by dividing two provinces Bengal and Panjab on the East and West ends of the north side of India, based on the Muslim population. They were called East- and West Pakistan respectively. Later on East Pakistan became an independent country named Bangladesh.

Panjab, instead of celebration, faced one of the worst crises in human history which is known as the riots of 1947. Borders between West Pakistan and East Panjab (part of India) were disclosed on the 15th of August and there was mass confusion among people. They did not know whether to stay or leave their homes. Soon after the borders were known, Muslims of West Pakistan started forcing Sikhs and Hindus out from their homes and businesses. Their homes and businesses were looted and people were killed and women were raped. There were killings in homes, buses and trains as people were moving to East Panjab. In retaliation, Sikhs forced Muslims out of their homes from East Panjab to go to West Pakistan. People on both sides lost their lives, homes, belongings and above all, their honor. They were called refugees (a hateful term at that time), it did not matter how honorable and important some of them were before the partition of India. They were to start their lives again. It was a very hard and enduring situation for them. The government later compensated them by allotting them vacated Muslim property such as homes and land according to their property in West Pakistan.

Both Dar Ji and Bi Ji's families suffered a great loss of their properties. Dar Ji's family lost their homes and property in Lyallpur and Bi Ji's family lost their business in Nankana Sahib. Luckily, Dar Ji had sold his home and property before the partition after moving to Hoshiarpur. Furthermore, the family suffered the tragic loss of Mohinder's Nana Ji, S. Ishar Singh Ji. He got sick and passed on Feb 16, 1947, before the partition of India. The family was devastated by this loss as he was the patriarch for the whole family, including his siblings. They all looked up to him for business guidance and his wisdom in general.

This tragedy affected Bi Ji's health in particular, she being the oldest of seven siblings was very close and loved by her dad. Bi Ji's poor health declined and she passed on in 1949, at the age of 33 years, leaving her 10 and 8 year-old daughters. Dar Ji was left with the responsibility to raise them by himself. Being a very close and caring family, Mohinder's grandmother, Jhaaiee Ji, moved in to take care of the girls and Dar Ji. Soon after, a mutually agreed marriage between Dar Ji and Bi Ji's Sister, Balbir Kaur, was arranged and finalized. It helped Dar Ji and the whole family to raise Mohinder and Malvinder under the best possible circumstances. Mohinder often told me how loving and exceptional the care was given by her Auntie (massi) now mother, addressed as Bhen Ji/Mama by Mohinder.

Dar Ji and Bhen Ji (Balbir Kaur)

Mohinder and Malvinder at age 10 and 8

This situation made it easier to endure the loss of Bi Ji. Bhen Ji has been an exceptionally caring and loving mother to Mohinder and Malvinder. She raised them and saw them through graduating from college, getting married and settling in as responsible adults. Nobody, including myself, could ever tell that Bhen Ji was Mohinder's maternal aunt rather than real mother. Everybody thought that she was the real mother. Furthermore, Bhen Ji had three of her own children, a daughter and two sons. They are named Upinder (Baby), Arvinder (Lovely) and Harinder (Tony). They are more than real sister and brothers to Mohinder and Malvinder. Their love and mutual respect is exemplary. They are always caring and sharing in all the family affairs. Mohinder loved and enjoyed them so much that her life became very happy and fulfilled.

Middle and High School

Mohinder continued her education from elementary to middle school and then to high school in the Gov. School for Girls, Hoshiarpur. Tenth grade was the final high school year. The final tenth grade exam is known as the Matriculation Exam. It was conducted by Panjab University. Each student is assigned a number called roll number which was used for each test rather than a student's name. The exam consisted of 5 different tests of subjects such as English, Math, Science and History. Math and English were considered important subjects. Students studied very hard for those. There used to be one test a day at a designated time all over the Panjab province. Tests were collected and sent to the designated undisclosed examiner at an undisclosed location. School Teachers had no input in the final grade. After a month or so results were published in the main provincial newspaper, Panjab Tribune, of successful candidates with their grade corresponding to their roll numbers. The matriculation grade determined the future college path of the student to pursue their career as medical, engineering, etc.

At that time, 1955, I was a graduate student preparing for my MSc degree in Zoology/Entomology. I was living with two of my friends almost next door to Mohinder's home. A mutual friend, Harbhajan Singh, a graduate student in Physics, whose sister, Bhupinder, was a friend of Mohinder and Malvinder, introduced me to Mohinder's family. He was living across the road from Mohinder's home. He asked if I could tutor Mohinder in Math and English for her to score higher on the Matriculation. I agreed and was formally introduced to the family.

After a few days, I started tutoring Mohinder. Mohinder knew most of the material really well as Dar Ji helped her, particularly in math. I was more helpful in English. Mohinder struck me as a very smart, well-mannered and self-respecting young girl. Besides our study topics, Mohinder did not talk much. Therefore, it was strictly tutoring. I could not dream that one day she would be my loving wife. She reminded me of my own younger sister, Nirmal, of about the same age as Mohinder. For tutoring, we used an octagonal hand-made beautiful wooden table with inlaid ivory work in the living room in front of a window. I tutored her for about a month.

The tutoring table

    Mohinder took the Matriculation Exam and passed with high marks with First Division (A grade). I went to visit the family to congratulate Mohinder for her hard work and success. Everyone was so happy with her achievement. After a week or so there was a graduation party and I was invited. Two of my classmates, Jagir Kaur and Rajinder Kaur were invited as well. We enjoyed the delicious food and the great company of the family members, Mohan auntie, Bhra Ji Avtar Singh and Malvinder. Especially presence of two of my dear friends, Baby and Lovely, who often came to visit and play with me in the evenings. They initiated the whole future relationship. Bhen Ji gave me a gift which was a brown piece of corduroy for pants. I used those corduroy pants for a long time.

I soon submitted my thesis for my Master's Degree, graduated with MSc. (Honor School) and left Hoshiarpur for Delhi in search of a job. Mohinder joined Panjab University College Hoshiarpur. Mohan auntie was already there finishing her college degree. Mohan auntie and two of her friends were very popular girls at the campus. She was known as Manmohan Arora. Mohinder had no problem at college being a niece of Manmohan Arora.

Chapter 3
COLLEGE EDUCATION

Mohinder joined Panjab University College Hoshiarpur, about a mile from her home, in 1955. She took art classes, philosophy and psychology, with a special interest in painting. She had two very close friends, Manjit and Nimmi, who were taking the same classes. They were together in college and after classes. They even ate together in each other's homes. They became lifelong friends.

With Manjit, Nimmi and sister Upinder

Mohinder graduated in 1957 from the junior college with an intermediate degree. At that time, I was working as an entomologist at Bombay Chemicals Pvt. Ltd, Bombay. After about six months in Bombay, I was awarded the Senior Research Fellowship by the Indian Council of Agriculture Research. The fellowship was for research towards a Ph.D. degree. I was to work at Panjab University College Hoshiarpur, under Dr. Hem Singh Pruthi, a renowned entomologist. The fellowship was a prestigious award from central government, and it was exciting to get back to Hoshiarpur and close to my family.

I resigned my job with Bombay Chemicals and came back to Hoshiarpur in March of 1957. One of my best friends and classmate, Sardul Singh, was still there and working towards his Ph.D. He offered me a room in his apartment which I took. After getting settled I started seeing my old friends. One evening, I went to see my old apartment and visited my dear friends Baby and Lovely playing outside their home. They were so excited to see me and started calling Veera Ji, Veera Ji (means brother dear). They took me in to see the family. It felt like home coming. I enjoyed the short visit and felt welcomed back. During this visit Jhaaiee Ji, Mohinder's grandmother, asked me, my reasons for coming back and about my family. I told her that I was awarded the fellowship for my Ph.D. and would be working at Panjab University College Hoshiarpur. She was pleasantly surprised. Then I told her about my farming small village and family. She asked me whether I was engaged or married yet. I said, "Neither of those as I am still studying." I did not give any serious thought to the talk and left. Furthermore, I had put on some weight, had grown up. My looks were more mature and my clothes and fashion were quite improved since I left Hoshiarpur in 1955.

Proposal

After a month or so, I was surprised when Dr. Guran Lal Arora, my Master's degree supervisor, called me into his office and asked me about my plans for marriage. I told him that I would begin to think about it after completing my doctorate. After about a week, he called me again into his office and said how about getting engaged while continuing your studies. I said, "I will give it a thought." He called me a third time to his office and this time there was another professor with him, Pro. Kulwant Singh, who was a very good friend of Mohinder's family and knew me too.

They asked me to sit down after greetings. I felt that there was something quite serious and it was. This time Dr. Arora said that I knew the family and the girl. After thinking a while I asked who was the family and the girl. At that Prof. Kulwant Singh said he would tell only if I would agree to get engaged. I responded by asking how I could be ready unless I knew the girl. Dr. Arora said, "Can we have your "yes" or "no" right now if we disclose the girl's name." Furthermore, if I said "no", they told me this matter should not leave the office for the sake of her family's honor. I gave my word of honor and they disclosed that girl was Mohinder of the Arora family. I could not believe it. I was overwhelmed and they could see it. It was unbelievable for a person like me coming from a small village and from a farming family to be engaged to Mohinder. Mohinder grew up to be a beautiful, well-mannered, very self-respecting, modest young lady. I told them that my answer was "YES", but that the final decision would depend on my parents' approval.

After a few days, I went to my village and told my mother about the proposal and about Mohinder and her family. She could not believe that her son, Darshan, was ready to get engaged. She went to Gurdwara Sahib to thank God and ask for His blessings. By that evening, my dad was told and he asked me to wait until he could learn more about the family and the girl. Ultimately, the relationship was approved and I gave the news to Dr. Arora. Mohinder's and my pictures were exchanged by the families so that relatives could see us for their approval and their blessings. Later, Bhen Ji told me that the proposal was initiated by her after I had come back from Bombay. I am forever grateful to her for this wonderful relationship.

Both our families were happy and the arrangements for the engagement were started. It was decided that ceremony should be in Hoshiarpur. The engagement date was decided and invitations were sent. Within a few days, I received my fellowship check from the government for three months. What a gift from God at the perfect time! It was enough money for the ceremony, ring and the party. My elder sister, Pritam Kaur, and I went to a well-known Jeweler in Hoshiarpur and bought an engagement ring with a blue stone for Mohinder.

Engagement

It was summer; therefore, the party was planned in the backyard of our apartment in Model Town, Hoshiarpur under a large rented tent with catered food. My supervisor, Dr. Pruthi, sent two of the lab assistants to help. They took over the arrangements. My father-in-law, S. Narinder Singh Ji with his relatives, including Baby, Lovely and one of their cousins came with ceremonial items such as fruit, sweets, a Gurbani Gutka (prayer book) and clothes, among other gifts. After prayers, the engagement ceremony was performed according to Sikh tradition. Then it was party time. It was a happy occasion attended by faculty members of the Zoology Department, our relatives and friends. It was a fun party with good food and celebration. All went wonderfully well with blessings for Mohinder and me from everyone. Dr. Arora was probably the happiest person, having accomplished his mission.

The same year, Mohinder started her bachelor degree studies in fine arts with painting as the major subject. As we both were studying in the same campus and Mohinder's art classes were in the same building (Zoology Department), we would sometimes cross each other while going to or coming from the building. Mohinder did not like it, and expressed her feelings to the family. Fortunately, I was offered an assistant Professor's Position at Khalsa College Amritsar, one of the prestigious colleges, with research facilities to continue my research. I accepted the position and joined Khalsa College Amritsar and moved to Amritsar in Aug. 1957. I cannot believe that I was so blessed by God with an amazing life partner and a job within six months of coming back from Bombay.

Mohinder continued her studies under congenial conditions for learning and fun with her friends. My dad suggested we wait at least two years before getting married so that we would be adequately mature, Mohinder could finish her degree, and our families would have enough time to be sure all was well and that they got along. Mohinder excelled in visual arts and painted quite a few beautiful paintings using an egg tempera medium technique. She competed in some important exhibitions and won awards particularly for the Kanga style of painting. She was awarded the first prize in painting in her final BA Exam. She graduated in 1959. At graduation, the Indian Defense Minister, Honorable B.K. Krishna Menon presented her award. Mohinder told me that at the presentation, the Defense Minister extended his hand for a hand shake, but instead of shaking his hand, Mohinder folded her hands and greeted him in a traditional Indian way. Mr. Krishna Menon smiled, folded his hands as well, congratulated Mohinder for her achievement and presented the award. Mohinder's appropriate manner brought applause from the audience.

Chapter 4
MOHINDER, THE ARTIST

Perhaps Mohinder discovered her talent as an artist from her art work in junior college. She realized that she had the potential to be a successful artist. Her art professor selected some of her paintings for exhibitions and encouraged her to further explore the field. She used pastel colors as her medium and produced some beautiful art work. Here are four of her Junior College paintings:

Bathroom items

Still Life

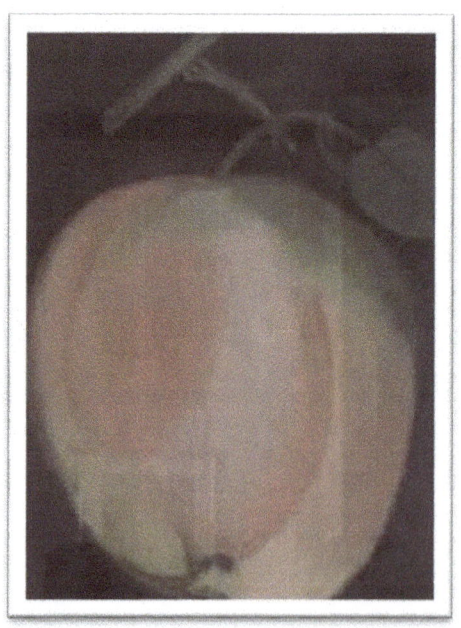

Peach

Mango

By the time she finished junior college she was ready to advance her talent further. Over the next two years, in college, she used egg tempera to paint some award-winning paintings such as "Moghul queen and her attendant lady", "desert queen", "Aasa Niraasa" (hope and despair), "a boat in the storm", "Buddha overlapped by Gandhi" (showing their philosophy of non-violence) and some more. Only the first two are still with us as the others were given to friends. Here are the first two:

Mughal Queen with the attendant

Queen in the Desert

Her passion for art spread and interested all three of our daughters. They took art classes in their school years. They turned out to be good artists. All of their paintings have been decorating our living and dining rooms over many years and different houses. We and all our guests enjoy these paintings.

One painting, the Strawberries, was our daughter, Sumandeep's high school assignment. Sumandeep was getting behind to finish it for the due date. The night before the due date, Mohinder helped her to finish this beautiful art work. More paintings done by Sumandeep are hanging in our dining room. Here are some of those:

Strawberries

Sumandeep's still life

Bina, our second daughter, is a very good artist as well. She did her self-portrait in high school, and later majored in art in her junior college. She is still pursuing abstract art.

Here is one of her art works:

Bina's Self Portrait

It is hanging on our living room wall.

Nina, our youngest daughter is also a very good artist. Some of her paintings are decorating our dining and living rooms as well. Here is one of those:

Nina's Dandelions

Bina and Nina organized an art club in their high school to share their interest in the art. It became a popular club with over twenty members. Both Bina and Nina served as its presidents. Visual arts are still pursued in our family. Both of Nina's daughters, Karuna and Anya, took art classes in high school and both are good artists with several of their art works decorating the walls of their home in Bangkok, Thailand. Karuna is majoring in art history in college and planning to make it her profession. Here are two of their art works:

Karuna's painting

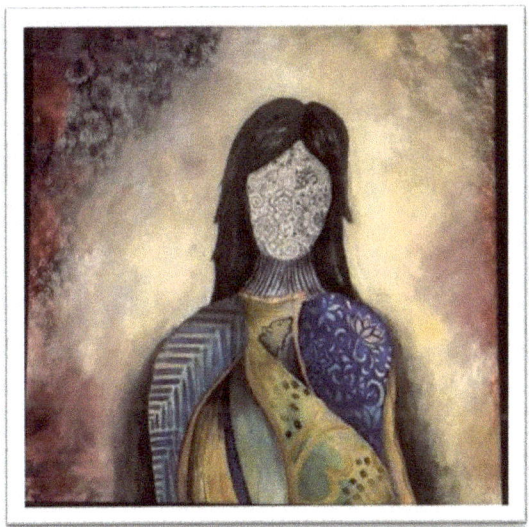

Anya's painting

Thus this art has become a family-wide interest which is an extension of Mohinder's passion for painting.

Chapter 5

WEDDING AND MARRIED LIFE

In 1959, Mohinder completed her B.A. at Panjab University College, Hoshiarpur. According to our plans, the marriage date was set for June 7, 1959. I was well settled in my job at Khalsa College Amritsar, ready to start our family life. Furthermore, by now, all my relatives at the village were happy with the relationship and all looked good. Both families had accepted each other and they looked forward to our marriage.

We decided to get married in Amritsar as most of Mohinder's relatives, my job and friends were there as well. Wedding preparations started on both sides. At my village, Jande Sarai, traditional songs were sung by women at our home every night for about two hours, followed by traditional snacks for about a month before the wedding. It was the customary way to publicize the wedding and announce the bride and bridegroom and their families to the village and neighboring villages. The only sad part was the absence of my mother at this special occasion. Both families wished that she was alive to bless us for a successful married life.

Wedding

On June 6, early in the morning I was given a special bath with a ceremonial scrub before dressing up in my wedding suit. The wedding party of about 50 people, consisting of at least one person from each family from the village and all my close relatives, was ready to proceed to Amritsar. We all went to the

Gurdwara Sahib, offered our prayer and asked for God's blessings for a successful wedding ceremony, and a fulfilling married life for the couple.

We started out from the village as a brass band played the traditional wedding music with drums and all. According to the village tradition my dad and uncles threw coins over me, which were picked up by the village children creating quite a scene. The band led us out of the village to Kartarpur. From there we took a train to Amritsar. Mohinder's family had arranged our stay in a historical building next to Santokh Sar and close to Sri Harmandir Sahib. There was a band and a beautifully decorated wedding mare for me to ride and all kinds of paraphernalia for the wedding party to proceed to the bride's place for the wedding-eve ceremony. I had a wedding suit, pink turban with a plume, and a decorated sword in my hand.

I rode the mare and the band played on when we arrived at the wedding place called Pashawarian -di-Dharmsala, a building in the vicinity of Sri Harmandir Sahib. Our party was received by Mohinder's family and friends with wedding songs. Prayers were offered for the union of our two families and traditional gifts were given by the bride's parents to my relatives. It was a great feeling for both the families. After the wedding reception, there was an elaborate and catered dinner hosted by Mohinder's family.

After dinner most of the party members visited Sri Harmandir Sahib, took a bath in the sacred Sarover and attended the evening services. Everybody enjoyed their pilgrimage in the holy city. The Sikh wedding ceremony (Anand Karaj) took place the next morning after breakfast. On June 7th both Mohinder and I, separately, paid homage at Sri Harmandir Sahib and took a bath in the Sarover. After breakfast, both families and friends gathered in a rather large wedding room with Sri Guru Granth Sahib Ji and Bhai Sahib (Sikh preacher) and Ragis (musicians) to perform the Sikh wedding ceremony.

Mohinder entered the room accompanied by her relatives. She was dressed in a beautiful reddish-orange traditional Panjabi wedding suite and bridal make up. She looked so beautiful. I was already sitting in front of the holy Sri Guru Granth Sahib Ji. Mohinder was seated by her dad at my side. The ceremony started with the Bhai Sahib explaining the responsibilities of both spouses in married life. Mohinder held one end of my sash and I held the other; Bhai Sahib then recited the first of the four stanzas of the Wedding Hymn (Lavan). Both of us bowed to Sri Guru Granth Sahib Ji in acceptance and walked around Sri Guru Granth Sahib Ji while the Ragis sang the same stanza.

We repeated this three more times with the recital and singing of the other three stanzas of Lavan. After Lavan, the first five stanzas and the last stanza of the song of bliss (Anand Sahib) were recited to finalize the marriage. At the end, we both were advised that marriage was a lifelong commitment and according to Sikhism, we should be so close in our thinking that it should feel like one spirit in two bodies. After the wedding both families celebrated the occasion with a catered dinner again hosted by Mohinder's family and we began our married life.

Mohinder's family gifted us with most of the essentials we needed to start a new household. There were gifts for me from Mohinder's family and for Mohinder from my family. All went very well, according to customs, we both were to return to my village after the wedding. Mohinder was accompanied by her maternal cousin, Tejinder Singh Arora, and my elder sister, Pritam Kaur. In the village, we were received by my family in a humble way due to the absence of dear Mother. After spending the night in the village, we went back to Amritsar to Mohinder's grandmother's home and stayed there for a few days. During that time, we were invited by Mohinder's relatives for dinner every day. Every time after dinner I was given a cash gift. We were treated like royalty by all the relatives.

Mohinder and Darshan

Visit to Simla

We visited Sri Harmandir Sahib to pay our respects and asked for blessings and guidance for our married life. After about a week we went to Hoshiarpur and enjoyed the same royal treatment there. After all these invitations and hospitalities, we went to Simla, a hill station, to escape the hot weather of the Panjab plains. It was a nice time getting to know each other better as life partners. In Simla, we met some of Mohinder's relatives who were, coincidently, there for summer vacation. They invited us for dinner and gave us money and gifts. The money came in handy for the trip.

In Simla, we had a great and memorable time together and began to know each other much more as a young couple. One day we went to see the shooting of a movie and saw some Bollywood stars, Dev Anand and Nutan, main characters of the movie. We rented bikes to go there which was fun to ride through the mountains. We had a picnic there and took some pictures in the beautiful mountains. Every day we planned a trip to the favorite sites around Simla and enjoyed each other's company. Mohinder was a fun lady to enjoy the trip with by trying different foods at different restaurants and particularly shopping. I loved the trip as I enjoyed the same things. I realized that we had a lot in common and that married life was going to be very enjoyable.

All went very well and we came back after a week to Amritsar to set up our new household. Right from the start, married life was so good with all kinds of social activities that I often wondered how I lived as a bachelor. I was always helped by my basic principle of living: firm faith in God, doing the right thing, and enjoying every phase of life. Mohinder turned out to be the same way. It always worked for us. I learned that Mohinder was a wonderful, very realistic and friendly person. It felt like we had known each other for a long time.

Khalsa College Amritsar

This college was established in 1892 by Sikh leaders, particularly Maharajas of various states such as Patiala, Nabha and Jeand in the Panjab Province, when India was under British rule. They were inspired by the teachings of the Sikh Gurus and thought about creating an institute to further the Gurus' teachings in the real sense. They donated all the money for the land and the buildings and a reserve fund for the maintenance of the buildings, grounds and staff salaries. The architecture is beautiful and one of a kind type of grand symmetrical, palace like buildings with domes and spacious beautiful playgrounds, lawns, hostels, a historical Gurdwara Sahib, housing for staff, a research agriculture farm, a dairy farm, and a lot more on the campus.

It sits on Grand Trunk (GT) Road on the west side of city of Amritsar, about twenty miles from Lahore, Pakistan. It occupies hundreds of acres of land between GT and Preet Nagar Roads. So far as academics were concerned, it taught students from Kindergarten to Master's and Doctorate degrees in certain subjects. Furthermore, it housed Panjab University's Botany Department which offered Masters, Ph.Ds. and postdoctoral research; the Sikh history research department; and a college for women offering a Bachelor degree in education.

It was all beyond my imagination, and I continued to learn that there was more to it. I enjoyed a special prestige due to the way I was offered the job.

Khalsa College Amritsar

We rented a small house, Ahluwalia Niwas, in Putli Gharh, which was within walking distance from my work. My brother, Jarnail Singh, was studying at Khalsa College and staying with us. To make it easier for Mohinder, my younger sister, Nirmal, came from the village and stayed with us for several months to keep Mohinder company and help her with the cooking and other daily chores. Mohinder and Nirmal became friends like two sisters.

I felt very lucky when I realized that Mohinder was an excellent cook. My mother was a great cook and now Mohinder too. Nirmal was also good at cooking. They were so happy being together in the kitchen. Within a few short months, Mohinder earned the respect of the Sarai family. Everybody liked her as much as her own side of the family did.

As hobby, Mohinder loved sewing, crocheting, and needle working. She used to sew some of her own dresses and used this creative pastime whenever needed. Being an artist, this outlet for her was an art work. One of her favorite items in the home was a good sewing machine.

We used to go to the movies and eat out. Mohinder made friends with two neighborhood families, one next door and the other across the street. One was a business man and the other a doctor. Both were very friendly young couples. The ladies, during their free time, used to get together.

Mohinder was quite daring too. We used to go for an evening walk after dinner. One late dark evening we were walking on a lonely street, when the street lights ended and the street seemed scary and spooky. I said, "Let us go back", but Mohinder wanted to go further. I stopped, and she continued. I waited a while and then followed her. She said that she was fine. I then realized that I had better agree with her in similar situations.

Furthermore, we visited our relatives quite often. Thus we as a new couple had a very good start. In fact, we expected our first baby within months of the marriage. Mohinder told me that she was not ready yet; however, I was excited to have a baby as I was 28 years old and I loved children.

We Became Parents

During the last three months of pregnancy, Mohinder stayed in Hoshiarpur and her Jhaaiee Ji came from Amritsar to help her. A female doctor took care of Mohinder during that time. She visited and checked on Mohinder. When summer vacation started, I came to Hoshiarpur to be with Mohinder for the new arrival. However, a day before the delivery, I had a telegram from my boss, the head of the Zoology Department, asking me to come back immediately to Khalsa College to conduct an exam. I was ready to decline the offer; however, Jhaaiee Ji convinced me to go to Amritsar. She was glad to get me out of the way as I would have been a hindrance rather than help during the delivery. The doctor was going to deliver the baby at home. On May 2, she delivered the baby. The baby was very special - the first grandchild for both families. Therefore, the best possible arrangements were made.

I went to Khalsa College and conducted the exam and visited some relatives. The next day, I got the news that I had become the father of a beautiful girl. She was formally named Sumandeep - a name suggested by my elder brother Pritam Singh. Sumandeep was later affectionately called by several names such as Mikky, Suman or Summu.

I came back to Hoshiarpur as an excited father with a "Johnson Baby Care Set" - a very expensive foreign item in those days. I could not believe it when I saw Sumandeep for the first time. She was so beautiful and such a delicate little baby. When I held her in my arms, I fell in love with her instantly. Mohinder's younger brother, Harinderpal (Tony) who was five at that time, became Sumandeep's caretaker and protector. He would stay and watch her most of the time and play with her tiny feet.

In the summer of 1960, I qualified for a residence on the campus which was on the second floor of the Patiala Hostel. Originally, it was used by the sons of Maharaja Patiala who had studied at Khalsa College. It was a comfortable and beautiful house with spiral stairs from the main ground entrance of the house and two small side doors on the back for convenience. There was a front veranda with a decorative grid and a semicircular bath with a hand pump. The middle part of the house had two very large (25 x 25 feet) rooms with a connecting door. One of them was used as a master bedroom and the other as a living room. It was a very comfortable and convenient home, only a few minutes walk from my department.

After summer break, we moved into our staff quarters. Again, my sister Nirmal Kaur, came and stayed to help us get settled. We furnished the home with new furniture, carpeting and other necessities to make our lives more comfortable. Mohinder made matching curtains and covers for the furniture. Our living room was decorated with art work and many of Mohinder's paintings. It looked like an art gallery. Besides lunch, I often came home to have a cup of tea and to relax between classes. Lots of other amenities came with the house, such as milk from the college dairy, grain from the college farm, laundry service, shoe polish service, and carry-out meals from the hostels - all at a very reasonable cost.

There were at least four permanent or part-time helpers doing different house jobs. For example, there was a cook named Jagdamba, Mikky's full time maid - a twelve-year-old girl named Raj, a kitchen cleaning lady, a janitorial lady to sweep the floors, and a washer man. There was always somebody in the house besides us family members. Life became very comfortable. Sumandeep became the center piece of the family. She was a beautiful and lovable good baby. We shared the responsibility of getting up during the night, as needed, for feeding and changing her, though she normally slept through the night. Every moment with her was enjoyable. We used to have evening walks with Sumandeep in a stroller. Sumandeep had a beautiful smile and we loved her baby talk.

We made some very good friends because of Sumandeep. All my colleagues loved her so much that they sometimes addressed us as Sumandeep's parents. She was talking and walking at the age of one. She was a beautiful, talkative doll. Her speech was clear with impressive vocabulary. In the Khalsa College staff quarters she became a role model for the other children of her age. She made us a busy and happy family. At her first birthday party many invited and some uninvited people came and had good food and a good time. The party was talked about and remembered for a long time. Mohinder and Mohan auntie planned the party and Mohinder's maternal aunties prepared some dishes, most talked about was the fish with mint sauce.

Mohinder and Mohan

Mohinder sewed Panjabi suites for Sumandeep. She used to curl Sumandeep's hair and dress her in those suites with matching shoes to go out for shopping or visiting friends and relatives. Sumandeep looked like a little model.

Trip to Srinagar, Kashmir

The Panjab University appointed me as an examiner for the Kashmir University Srinagar to conduct a practical exam in May 1962 for premedical students at Srinagar, the capital of Kashmir state. I accepted the one-week assignment which meant extra money and a fun place to visit. Furthermore, examiners were treated very well as the results of the premedical students depended partly on the lab exam. I asked Mohinder to accompany me as Srinagar and its surroundings were very beautiful and in the middle of the Himalaya Mountains. She agreed and we took Sumandeep to Hoshiarpur to stay with Mohinder's family. We took a bus to Srinagar. It was a great trip through winding roads in the mountains with breathtaking beauty. We saw snow on the ground for the first time. We were a party of four professors from Khalsa College with similar assignments, along with Mohinder and another lady.

In Srinagar we stayed in a houseboat on a river. It was a fun place to stay and an interesting experience to sleep on a bed rocked by the wind and the flowing water. We shopped from vendors in their small boats visiting from morning to evening. After a few hours of work, we used to, almost every afternoon, go for shopping and enjoy ourselves in the Srinagar bazaars. For dinner almost every evening we were invited by professors of the Kashmir University or relatives living in Srinagar. The rest of the time we would go sightseeing at surrounding attractions like the historical gardens of Mughal Emperor Jahangir who used Srinagar as his summer capital. We also visited places like Pehalgam, Gulmarg and Khilanmarg up in the mountains. From Gulmarg, we rode horses to Khilanmarg as it was quite a steep and hilly trail. Mohinder's horse was the best and with a beautiful and proud rider. After reaching the Khilanmarg we found ourselves surrounded by snow. There we played in the snow like little kids. We had lots of fun as it was our first time experiencing it. At the top, there was an Indian Army post and a restaurant run by a Sikh army officer. He was a courteous and delightful host. He served us lentil soup (daal) and rice for one rupee per serving. It tasted delicious.

On the Himalayan snow

One night around midnight while on the house boat in Srinagar, Mohinder woke me up and asked to go back to Hoshiarpur. I, while half- asleep, asked why? She said that in her dream she saw Sumandeep very sick and asking for her Mama. I tried to calm her down but she was serious and determined to leave in the morning. I convinced her to stay as only two more days of exam were left. She agreed but still she was sad. After the exams, we left Srinagar for Amritsar by bus. About half of the way at Gurdaspur junction, one route went to Hoshiarpur and the other to Amritsar. Mohinder decided to go to Hoshiarpur. She was serious and took the bus to Hoshiarpur. I went to Amritsar to report to work. When I went to Hoshiarpur at the end of the week I could not believe it, but Sumandeep was very sick with measles. Mohinder said that she knew. I believed her and her motherly instinct.

Sumandeep was everybody's favorite due to her charming personality, diplomatic, and affectionate behavior. Once, some of my friends came to visit me; they knocked at the door and continued talking while waiting for me. Sumandeep heard the knocking, answered the door, and greeted them. They apparently ignored her and continued their conversation. Sumandeep politely invited them in. They did not pay any attention to the little hostess. After waiting a while, she spoke a little louder and invited them in and offered them tea. It did not work either. Sumandeep was not happy with their behavior and said rather clearly and a little loudly, "If you don't want to come in and have some tea then why don't you leave." It got their attention immediately; they stopped talking and felt bad about ignoring Sumandeep. They nicely asked Sumandeep about me. When I came to the living room, they were busy talking to Sumandeep. They told me the whole story and how impressed they were with Sumandeep's hospitality.

Family picture

Another time we had a new radio in the bedroom and a speaker in the kitchen. One day, Mohinder was working in the kitchen and listening to Indian movie songs on the radio. At the end of a program, she asked Sumandeep to turn off the radio. Sumandeep turned off the radio and Mohinder asked if she turned the radio off. Sumandeep looked at the speaker in the kitchen and said, "Yes, Mama, you should have known from the kitchen speaker." Mohinder hugged her and was impressed with her presence of mind. Sumandeep was mostly a leader among children of her age group and even a little older. Her absence in the house, even for a short time, was felt a lot. Wherever she went, she became a favorite of almost everyone. She was a very diplomatic charmer for all of us and our friends. She was treated like royalty and she behaved like royalty as well.

My brother Pritam Singh sent a puppy, a mixed breed between a beagle and a terrier, for Sumandeep from Delhi. We named him Jigi. Sumandeep loved the dog and treated him like a real person. Some of her favorite things were feeding Jigi, taking him out for a walk, and putting make-up powder on him.

Life at Khalsa College became comfortable, very enjoyable and socially fulfilling. However, educationally speaking I was feeling stagnant, and it was scary to think that I would be spending the rest of my career life at Khalsa College teaching the same classes like some old professors were doing.

As the teaching became easier, I had more time to spend with my family and in the staff room to read newspapers and visit with colleagues from other departments. Some of them started their career quite young and were getting old by then. One day an old colleague made a remark, "Khalsa College is like an open, comfortable, and sweet prison; once you are in it often times you would never leave it until you retire." His statement made me think that I should get out and complete my Ph.D. in some foreign university before it was too late. Dad's wish for me to get an education in a foreign country also came to my mind. Jarnail Singh's education was progressing well enough for him to graduate in spring of 1962. I thought that if things worked out, I could start my higher education in 1963.

Jarnail Singh graduated and got a teaching job in a newly opened college. I became more serious about my higher education. I talked to my family about my desires and received a good response. I wrote letters to the American and Canadian Embassies in New Delhi and asked for a list of Universities offering Ph.D. programs in applied entomology, their addresses, and contact persons. Within a couple of months, I got from both the embassies lists of universities offering the degree I wanted. I picked ten well known universities and wrote them about my interest in admission and financial aid. Most of them wrote back; however, I received favorable response from only four universities. Even those did not offer any readily available financial aid due to already being committed to other graduate students.

The University of Alberta, Edmonton gave me admission as a provisional candidate for the Ph.D. and promised financial aid after the first semester, provided my grades were satisfactory. After a year, I would be considered for Ph.D. candidacy depending upon my academic performance. I got a detailed breakdown of all the expenses such as tuition, books, lodging and boarding. It all came to about 500 dollars per month. Compared with Indian currency, it was too expensive and everything was about five times more expensive than the Indian standard. I was not happy about the whole situation.

I wanted to go and take a chance, but a comfortable life at Khalsa College was not easy to let go. Furthermore, I was to leave my dear family behind at least until I was set in studies and financially able to support them.

We did not have enough money saved even for one year's expenses at the University of Alberta. To make the things worse, Khalsa College would not give me a three to five year leave of absence, the time needed to complete the Ph.D. work. However, I still wanted to take a chance. My department head advised me against going abroad. He said, "Darshan, you are almost lined up to become the head of the department because I will be retiring in a few years. You cannot have a better job than the one you have, even after completing your Ph.D." His wife was a good friend of Mohinder's. She advised Mohinder that it would be a mistake for me to leave such a good job and jump into an unknown situation. Mohinder was mostly supportive of me but this time it seemed to be too big of a step into the unknown. She discussed the matter with her friends and relatives, but no one had a clear answer. She was always very realistic. To explain her feelings she made a remark that in her fate there were only two things: The sand of rainy season streams (Chooas) of Hoshiarpur and the dust of Amritsar streets. It meant that we were not going anywhere, and should forget about foreign travels. I responded, "One cannot know without taking a chance."

I was seriously thinking the whole situation over when Dad came from the village to visit us. He asked me about my serious mood. I told him about the admission to the University of Alberta and all the rest of the situation. He was very happy about the admission. He advised me, "Son, you can borrow money but you cannot borrow time. Therefore you should go and avail the opportunity." I told Dad that our savings were not enough to get me through for the first year of my studies. He responded that I could borrow from him. I was surprised and asked how and when I would pay him back. He replied, "Darshan, don't worry about it, you may pay whenever you can; otherwise pay me by supporting your children in their education. That is how." For Dad, education for children was the best investment one could make. It was a great and encouraging feeling. Mohinder was told by some of her friends that a few of their relatives went to Canada for higher education and were still struggling to finish their Ph.D. studies even after five years. Finally she agreed and I started planning to go to the University of Alberta, Canada for higher education.

Leaving India

I wrote a letter to the University of Alberta, Edmonton, stating that I would be joining the University for Graduate Studies in the fall of 1963. Promptly, the university responded with detailed information about the school, tuition, and expenses for boarding and lodging. It gave me only a little over a month to get ready. To start with, I needed a passport from the Indian Government, a visa from the Canadian Embassy, and an airline ticket from a travel agency. Delhi was the closest city to get all that done.

I went to Delhi, and stayed with my brother, Pritam Singh. He was a great help in getting these things done. I applied for a passport and started shopping around for an airline ticket from a travel agency. For the money exchange for the first year's expenses, I needed about five hundred Canadian dollars and a permit for the exchange from the Reserve Bank of India for the rest of my stay in Alberta. Everything went smoothly and worked out within a week or so. I got a student visa from the Canadian Embassy and the money exchange permit from the reserve bank of India, which was probably the most difficult.

I came back to Amritsar, gave my resignation to Khalsa College, and started packing. Mohinder decided to take Sumandeep and move to Hoshiarpur to stay with her parents until she could join me in Canada. We planned for Mohinder and Sumandeep to join me and visit Canada before my graduation and return to India.

Farewell to the Family

On September 15, 1963 we left Amritsar by train for Delhi. My dad, brothers, sisters, nieces, nephews and in-laws were waiting for us at the Jalandhar railway station. It was a joyous farewell party with food brought by my in-laws from Hoshiarpur. After a quick dinner and fun party, it was time to leave. Dad and I left Jalandhar for Delhi, while Mohinder and Sumandeep went to Hoshiarpur. I bade good-bye to my family with tears in my eyes and a choked throat. Dad looked at me and said, "Son, everything is going to be alright. Unless we take chances in life, we can never achieve our visions or dreams." It was great to have Dad with me.

We reached Delhi the next morning and my brothers, Pritam Singh and Jarnail Singh, were waiting for us. The same afternoon, I purchased my airline ticket from a travel agency and was ready for the rest of the trip. The next day, I was to leave for Calcutta and visit relatives on the way in Agra. Again at the Delhi railway station Dad, brothers, Pritam Singh and Jarnail Singh, were there to see me off. I hugged my brothers, and Dad, and asked him for parting advice. He responded, "Son, by now, you know all I had to teach you and more due to your education." I asked again politely, he looked at me and smiled and said, "If you insist, here is my advice: you will be representing our family and our traditions in Canada; represent them well. Secondly don't get materialistic at the cost of your family; don't make Mohinder work until the children are grown up and in school. Mohinder's loving care and training for children should be the first priority." I nodded in the affirmative and hugged Dad. Then he said, "Son, you will be back before you know it and I will be waiting for you." I left with tearful eyes. At that, my brother Jarnail Singh said, "Don't be sad because I will follow you soon."

Flight to Canada

After visiting relatives in Agra, I took the train to Calcutta. I was on my own from that point on. I stayed overnight in a hotel in Calcutta, one of the biggest cities in India. My plane left the next day for Vancouver, Canada, via Hong Kong. There was a lot of anxiety about the unknown going through my mind. For travel from Vancouver to Edmonton, I had two choices either by air or by train. I went with the train to enjoy the Canadian Rockies. With a strong faith in God and my attitude, I was ready to face the challenge of the unknown.

Chapter 6
UNIVERSITY OF ALBERTA, EDMONTON, CANADA

Edmonton

I reached Edmonton the next day in the early afternoon, put my luggage in a locker, and took a taxi to the University of Alberta. The driver dropped me in front of the Agriculture Building which housed the Entomology Department. I introduced myself to the secretary of the Entomology Department and she informed Dr. Brian Hocking, the head of the Entomology Department, about me. He called me in and was surprised to see me. He asked me how I got to Edmonton and the department without informing them. I told him by taxi. He said "All the way from Amritsar?" with a smile. I responded, "From the Edmonton Railway Station." It was a good start. He was impressed with my being innovative and independent. He told me most foreign students needed help from the department for transportation from the airport and lodging until they got settled.

Dr. Hocking asked me which graduate courses I would like to take for the first semester. I responded, any of the required courses. At that he said that he would like to give me a placement exam to determine the courses. I agreed and he started the exam with questions about Zoology, Entomology, and Ecology, knowing my educational background and teaching experience. Apparently, I passed the exam. Dr. Hocking decided the courses for me as Biometrics, Biochemistry, and German language. I did not have any idea about these courses. Besides that, I was to do research on my dissertation project. It seemed hard but I was determined to learn and study. Dr. Hocking then took me to the secretary for any assistance with lodging and boarding arrangements.

I asked the secretary if there were any other students in the department from Panjab. She smiled and said there was a herd of them in the Agriculture building and some in the Entomology and Zoology Departments. I asked their names. She mentioned Som Dutt Sharma, Sohan Singh Jande, and some others.

I just could not believe it. I knew both Som Dutt and Sohan Singh. In fact they were my friends from the Panjab University; especially Sohan Singh who was one of my best friends. Som Dutt was a year senior and Sohan Singh was a year junior from me. They both were graduate students. Som Dutt was in the Entomology Department and Sohan Singh was in the Zoology Department.

The secretary called Som Dutt on the intercom and informed Sohan Singh on the phone about my arrival. In a few minutes both of them came and we had an unexpected and pleasant reunion. None of us knew about the coincidental situation. Both of them offered to let me stay with them until I found my own place. I felt good being with my old friends in Edmonton and thanked God for all this.

That night, I stayed with Sohan Singh and learned about University life and living in Edmonton. The next day, I went to the University, bought books and talked to Som Dutt about his boarding and lodging arrangement. He told me that he was staying in a home and paying 60 dollars/month for board and lodging where the service was great, and the land-lady, Mrs. Talbot, was a wonderful person.

Meeting Mrs. Talbot

I liked the arrangement and asked Som to ask Mrs. Talbot if she had a room for me too. Som called her, and I was surprised to learn that she had a vacancy. She invited me for dinner and to see the room. Mrs. Talbot served us an impressive dinner with baked chicken as the main dish and blueberry pie as the dessert. There were six graduate students, and Mr. and Mrs. Talbot at the dinner table. Besides the main dishes, dinner was complete with salad, dinner rolls, and baked potatoes. I enjoyed the dinner and the hospitality of Mrs. Talbot. Then she gave me a tour of the house and showed me the vacant room.

The room had a window and a small closet. It was furnished with a single bed, a desk and a chair. The bath room was shared with other boarders. I took the room and Mrs. Talbot explained the house rules, such as no girlfriends, no drinking, and no smoking in the house. I accepted the rules. She looked at me inquisitively and asked if I had any food preference. I told her that I would let her know in the morning. I moved into my room the same night.

After the evening prayer, I thanked God for all his blessings for taking such good care of me in Canada, with old friends like Som Dutt and Sohan Singh, and a person like Mrs. Talbot in such a short time. When I thought about the food preference, I decided I would be happy with whatever was served. It would be easy for Mrs. Talbot. With my background, I did not like eating pork or beef at that time; otherwise the whole weekly menu (posted in the dining room) was very good. My favorite part of a meal was salad, side dishes, and dessert. Furthermore, I did not like to burden Mrs. Talbot with extra planning, shopping, and cooking for me separately.

In the morning when I came down for breakfast, Mrs. Hilda Talbot was standing close to the stairs and waiting for my answer about the food preference. I looked at her smiling face and said, "Mrs. Talbot, I will eat whatever you will serve." She was so happy to hear that. She gave me a warm motherly hug and said, "Son, we will get along just fine." I responded to "Mom" (Mrs. Talbot's affectionate name used by the boarders) with thanks for having me as a boarder. Mom was in her late 60s with arthritis. She was a caring and compassionate lady earning her living by taking care of six graduate students and her husband. She was an inspiration for me.

Student Again

Thus I was set for studies. It was a very warm feeling as I had a place to stay and Som as my walking companion to the University which was about fourteen blocks from Mrs. Talbot's home. Next day I started classes. All my courses were strange to me, and I felt that I did not know much about any one of them.

I wrote to Mohinder and Dad about all my experiences. They were happy that I was all set in Edmonton. To stay occupied, Mohinder took some classes at Panjab University College and got Sumandeep enrolled in a nearby kindergarten school. Thus the whole family was back to school. After that, we had weekly correspondence through letters.

Financial Help

After two weeks of my being in Edmonton, Sohan Singh asked if I could teach two, two hour Zoology Labs per week to the class he was teaching for eighty dollars per month. I happily agreed as I had taught Zoology for six years at Khalsa College Amritsar text and lab. It was an easy job for me. I needed money to pay the rent. My financial worries were over and I could concentrate on my studies. I was feeling more than ever the strength of faith and the power of prayer working for me.

I wrote to Mohinder about it and mentioned that hopefully I would get more financial aid soon to support the family and we would be together in Edmonton. Knowing this, Mohinder was happy and we were looking forward to be together again.

Edmonton Weather

Edmonton was very cold, so cold that some mornings in the winter months were too cold. Sometimes the temperature ranged from -30 to - 50 degrees F. although, I had warm clothing, such as sweaters, jackets, and an overcoat. Still those were not warm enough for the Edmonton weather. So I bought some warm clothing and tried to get used to the cold weather with snow, sleet, and ice everywhere.

Som Dutt and I used to walk to the University. While walking to the university sometimes moisture from my breath would freeze on my beard and mustache. By December 1963, winter had really set in with blizzards, snow storms, and freezing rains. The land was white with snow and looked like a Christmas picture from a magazine. For me it seemed like it was always night as we walked to the university in the dark and walked back in the dark. The sun used to rise and set when we were still in class. It was a strange feeling to be in the dark almost all the time. On December 22, there was almost no day as there was not much time between sunrise and sunset. It was the longest night and shortest day and very different than India.

While getting used to all that, I was struggling and trying to understand all three courses. I realized the grading system was different than that of India and the final grade was formed of only a certain percentage of each test. Furthermore, exams were mostly multiple choices.

Therefore, it took me about a month to start making decent grades; for example in Biochemistry the grade jumped from 48 to 84 percent in the second exam.

Biometrics was the same way. German language was a pass/fail course. Graduate students were required to translate satisfactorily a scientific article from German to English. We could take the final test twice. Thus I concentrated on Biochemistry, Biometrics and the research project.

A Valuable Lesson

While I was adjusting to the new environment, missing my family and my comfortable life in India, Dr. Hocking asked me to turn in, by the next Thursday, a five to six page report on my research work done in India. I responded, "Sir, I am too busy with my studies; therefore, I will submit the report if I will have time." At that, Dr. Hocking looked at me and said, "I beg your pardon, young man." He was very serious. He told me, "Everyone has only twenty four hours in a day and it is a matter of managing the time. Never ever say, if I will have time." After that he said he would like to have the report at 9AM sharp the next Monday rather than Thursday. I got the message and learned a very valuable lesson. I worked hard that weekend, finished my assignments, and finalized the research report. I was in Dr. Hocking's office at 8:45 AM Monday. He looked at the report, smiled and said, "Well done, Darshan." I sobered up in a hurry from being a Professor from Khalsa College Amritsar to a student at the University of Alberta.

Student Life

Mom used to do all my laundry, starched my turbans, cleaned my room, and packed my lunch. It was all part of sixty dollars per month charges. Thus I had only one thing to do: Study. By March, 1964 weather was warmer, snow was disappearing, and I was adjusted to my studies. I used to go through all my class notes and rewrite them with the help of textbooks to have a clearer understanding of all the material being covered during the day. This helped me to be ready for the next day's lessons. Quite often, it used to be midnight or 1 AM before I would go to sleep. I figured out that five to ten minute naps were very refreshing whenever I felt sleepy or tired during study.

My grades were good enough in first semester that Dr. Hocking gave me a teaching assistant position in the Entomology Department. With the position, I was able to apply for Mohinder and Sumandeep to join me in Canada. Dr. Hocking was concerned that my studies might be affected by my family's being with me. I assured him that I would be able to study even better if my family were with me. Dr. Hocking gave me a letter stating that I had the teaching assistantship which was enough to support my family in Canada. With the help of his letter and other support documents, Mohinder and Sumandeep got their visas for Canada.

It took Mohinder about a month in Delhi to get clearance from the Indian Government to travel to Canada. They came via Thailand where Mohan auntie was living. They stayed with Auntie for a month before coming to Edmonton. In the meantime Mom had rented an apartment for us just next door to her. She thought that she could help the family get adjusted to Canadian life and could also help in baby-sitting Sumandeep. Until the family came, I ate at Mom's and slept in our apartment. Mom wouldn't let me cook and waste time which could affect my studies. Furthermore, she used to stock the apartment refrigerator with groceries every week hoping Mohinder would feel at home after joining me. At the end of the week, she would stock the refrigerator with fresh groceries and use the old ones. She gave me some china and pots and the rest, we needed, she helped me to buy. We shopped for winter coats for Mohinder and Sumandeep. I was all ready for my family to join me.

Family Arrived

It was already Oct, 1964 and getting cold in Edmonton. The day when the family was to arrive in Edmonton, I checked with the airlines and asked about Mohinder Sarai as a passenger on the specified flight. They told me that nobody of Sarai name was on the flight as Mohinder used her first name only. As Mom was to take me to the airport, she said that unless I was sure about Mohinder's arrival, there was no sense in going to the airport in this cold weather. She said we should wait until we knew for sure. I was sad to wait and my phone rang quite often. Every time, one of my friends was calling to inquire about Mohinder's arrival. Then suddenly I got the most pleasant call with Mohinder's voice asking why I was not at the airport to receive them. I explained the reason and was so excited to hear Mohinder's voice. I called Mom and told her that they already had arrived at the airport. Mom came right away to pick me up, and she drove as fast as she could. We apologized to Mohinder for being late. I hugged them and apologized for the mix up. It was a very exciting moment. I picked up Sumandeep and had a big hug from her. She said, "I love you Daddy." It was so sweet and loving to hear that. She was quite grown up in a year. It was a cold evening with snow on the ground, a new experience for Sumandeep.

Mom loved the family and instantly got attached to Sumandeep, the charmer. Mom used to baby-sit Sumandeep, and Sumandeep loved to be with Mom. They would bake cookies together. It was very interesting to watch them talk. At first Sumandeep would communicate only in Panjabi, then some English and the rest Panjabi, but in about a month Sumandeep switched to English mostly. In the course of their communication, Mom learned some Indian words. Somehow, they communicated quite effectively. Sumandeep was a fast learner and quite a talker. Most of my Indian friends admired her manners and Panjabi vocabulary. She was a role model for the other Indian children.

Before my family joined me, I had cleared most of the course work. For German, I had to retake the exam. Finally, I passed German with the remark from the examiner that he seldom expected such a good translation from a graduate student. I asked him to please write that down on the result sheet, which he did. My supervisor, Dr. Evans, was pleased to see that. After passing German, my concentration was on research work.

Research Work

For field research work, I found a site about twenty miles outside Edmonton around an area known as Atim Creek. There were wheat fields and pastures infested with a cricket, Nemobius fasciatus, which became my research insect. My research project was to determine the adaptation of the cricket to the winter conditions of the Edmonton region. Research required lab experimentation and field work to study the insect in nature.

For the field work, with the help of Mom, we bought a used 1954 Chevrolet Belaire, sedan, for $190, from a graduate student from India, who was going back after his graduation from the Engineering Department. The car was red with white trim and standard shift. Mom, after driving, told me that it was a good car for that price. Mohinder and Sumandeep were happy. We got the insurance from Mom's insurance agent. After that I had driving lessons from a driving instructor. It was quite an experience including a fender bender (accident) soon after I had my first driving lesson.

We came back after a dinner with a friend, I suddenly had the urge to drive the car. I asked Mohinder about driving the car around the block. She hesitantly agreed. Our car was parallel parked with a car in front and one behind. We got in the car and I started the engine, put it in the first gear, turned the wheels and took my foot off the break. Our car hit the bumper of the front car, crossed the street, and hit a tree and stopped. We were shocked. Then Mohinder quietly got out of the car and went in with Sumandeep. Neighbors came out and saw the accident. I asked Mom for help. She asked the neighbor, owner of the damaged car, not to report the accident to the police or his insurance company, just to get the estimate in the morning and we would pay for the damage. The next day our neighbor called and told me that estimate was $120, which I paid him. I apologized to Mohinder for my being impulsive and she said, "Thank God nobody got hurt." We thanked God that it was not too bad. I thanked Mom and said that I learned my lesson.

Within a couple of days after the accident, our landlord came by and noticed our car with the bent fender. I told him about the accident. Later he called and said, "Darshan bring your family at the week end and have dinner with us and I will fix your car." We went to his house and they had grilled chicken for dinner which we enjoyed. He had already had a fender from the salvage yard and had it painted matching our car. He replaced the fender. We thanked him and asked about its price. He responded that it was a gift from him to us. It was unbelievable how fortunate we were to have friends like him.

In about two months, I got my driver's license and started driving around. It was so nice to be independent. Besides shopping and field visits, we started going to various parks, visiting friends, and going to lakes. Our social life was great with some of my old friends and new friends. Mohinder and Sumandeep became a part of the Indian community in and around Edmonton in a short time. For me it was great, a congenial and happy situation to study and do my research work.

Mohinder adapted to the Canadian life style and food quite quickly. She did not have any problem with the language either and felt quite at home in Canada. She enjoyed Canadian dishes, and learned Canadian cooking from Mom. She loved cold cut meats such as turkey and ham to make sandwiches. She got used to being independent without servants. Thus we had more time with the family without helpers around. We were quite often either inviter or invitee for dinners and picnics with friends. Our Indian friends were mainly formed of some visiting professors from the Panjab University, a Panjabi professor from the political science department and some teachers working in the rural towns around Edmonton. Their families loved to have their children meet and be friends with Sumandeep.

At white mud Creek Park

At Saskatchewan River

In Edmonton Home

With our first car, Chevy

At the University of Alberta

Edmonton home backyard

When free, ladies used to get together for shopping, etc. Mom often took Mohinder for shopping and helped her in Canadian cooking. They became very good friends in a short time. For entertainment we bought a used black and white console television. Sumandeep loved to watch cartoons and we loved to watch week end movies and programs such as Walt Disney and the Andy Griffith Show. Our family was quite happy and adjusted to the Canadian life style. Dr. Hocking invited us in 1964 for a Christmas dinner and party, and introduced the Sarai family to the Faculty staff and students. One of my professors said, "Darshan, you have a beautiful family and now I realize why you were missing them so much."

Another Tragedy

All was moving forward quite smoothly, when I got a telegram from my brother Pritam Singh that Dad had passed on suddenly. He wrote that Dad got up early in the morning and walked about seven miles to visit one of his elder sisters. Then he walked to Jalandhar to meet our brother Karnail Singh and took care of some court business. Then they both walked to village, Nagre, to visit his youngest sister and daughter. While walking, he started having chest pain. A doctor came from Jalandhar, checked and gave him some medicine. Dad passed on the same night. Like Mother, Dad passed on quickly and peacefully after meeting all those relatives by walking. It was very sad for the family, especially for me. My dreams to go back to India after graduation and spending time with Dad were shattered. I could not accept the fact that Dad had passed away. I could not concentrate on my studies. We grieved and Mohinder helped me endure the loss and carry on to fulfill Dad's dreams. Faith to accept God's Will helped me and my family to endure the loss. Dad's teachings and loving memories became more cherished and a contributing guiding light in my life.

Candidacy/Comprehensive Exam

In the spring of 1965, I had completed all the requirements for the comprehensive/candidacy exam for my Ph.D. This exam determined whether the student would be a candidate for the doctoral degree or not. Failing the exam meant another master's degree. So it was considered one of the hardest and the most important exams. The exam was normally a three or four hour oral exam conducted by six examiners from different departments related to the research project of the candidate.

Mohinder helped me in the preparation for the exam by listening to me. Surprisingly, she knew a lot just by listening. Whenever I was not clear in my answer she would tell me. I would go back to my notes to check the answer. Most often Mohinder was right. I asked her, "How did you know?" She replied, "By listening to you and from your face." It was an interesting piece of team work.

I was ready for the exam to the point that I stopped studying three or four days before. During that time, we went to a movie and a picnic in the park with a friend and his family. If a question came to my mind and I was not sure about the answer, I simply looked into my notes.

On the exam day, I got up early, had a shower, prayer and a light breakfast. Mohinder wished me good luck and I walked to the university. I entered the exam room; all of the examiners were already there. They introduced themselves and the exam started as a round table with a couple of questions from each examiner. I remember some of those questions such as a Zoology professor took a bone specimen from his pocket and asked me to identify that. I said, "Sir, it is 5th cervical vertebra of a cow." He was amazed with my answer and was satisfied. Another examiner from the Zoology Department asked me to identify a specimen mounted in a plastic block. I said, "It is an Ascidian, commonly known as a sea squirt, and it is a chordate." He was satisfied too. Dr. Hocking asked me who Erasmus Darwin was, and his most important contribution to the field of Biology. I answered, "Erasmus Darwin was grandfather of Charles Darwin and his most important contribution to Biology was Charles Darwin." At that Dr. Hocking smiled and remarked, "Darshan, you stole that answer from my head." I said, "Sir, because I am your student." The rest of the questions were relatively easy and I was quite confident about most of the answers. Dr. Hocking looked at every body and asked if there were any further questions. Everyone was seemingly satisfied.

Dr. W.G. Evans, my supervisor, signaled me to leave the room so the committee could make their decision. He closed the door. In about ten minutes, Dr. Evans came out smiling and asked me to come in. When I entered the room all the examiners congratulated me for passing the exam. Dr. Hocking shook my hand and remarked "Very well done, Darshan." Both Drs. Hocking and Evans were very happy and proud of me.

I called Mohinder and gave her the good news. After that I called Mom and told her too. They were very happy. Thus I was one step closer to getting the doctorate degree. All I needed was to finish the research work, submit a dissertation (thesis), and to pass the final oral exam in defense of the dissertation.

For celebration we planned a trip to Jasper and Banff National Park with a friend, Didar Singh, a teacher and his family, wife and two daughters. He bought a new car and wanted to test it by going on a trip. We drove to Jasper stayed overnight, and the next morning after breakfast we visited Athabasca Falls and other close by sites. These falls are fantastic and very wide. Mohinder took quite a few pictures and was so happy at the gorgeous view of the falls. In the afternoon we drove through the beautiful Rockies to Banff.

In the Rockies

We reached Banff in the evening. After walking around and enjoying the night scene of the city, we stayed overnight in a hotel. After breakfast we took a Gondola ride to a ski resort with a restaurant on the top of the mountain. It was a beautiful view of the city and surrounding area such as Lake Louise and peaks around it. We had our lunch up there. In the afternoon we visited Lake Louise surrounded by seven high peaks of the Rockies. After that, we drove to Calgary and stopped at Dinosaur Park. Then headed back to Edmonton. It was a great and memorable first trip of ours from Edmonton to the Rocky Mountains. Mrs. Didar Singh was like a sister to Mohinder. Their daughters, one almost of Sumandeep's age, had fun together. Everybody enjoyed the trip which went very well.

Sumandeep's fifth birthday was another exciting event for the Sarai family. Mohinder with the help of Mom planned a birthday party with balloons, cake and other food items both Indian and Canadian. Sumandeep invited her friends, most of them Panjabi and some Canadian. Veenu, daughter of my friend Sohan Singh, stole the show. She was so happy and dancing around making everyone laugh. She was only a year or so younger than Sumandeep. The weather was pleasant, warm and sunny. All the guests enjoyed the party. Now Sumandeep was ready to go to Kindergarten School.

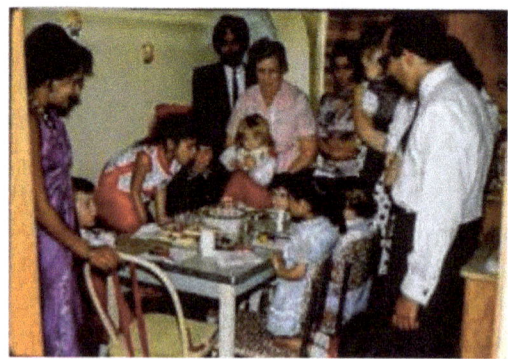

Sumandeep's fifth birthday party

Research and Dissertation

My research progressed well and I was feeling confident enough to have some more fun time with the family. In Edmonton region, June 21 is the longest day and the shortest night. Seemingly there is almost no night as sunset light was followed by the dawn light in a very short time. Mostly people celebrated this evening as an outdoor picnic or cook out. We too, with some friends, did the same. It was another interesting experience for us.

In October, 1965, Dr. Evans checked my research work with analyzed experimental data. He told me that the research was sufficient to write the dissertation. I said that the work would make only about one hundred typed pages. He said, "We need quality and not quantity." It was great news.

In December, 1965, I started writing the dissertation. Sumandeep was going to a nursery school. One of our very close friends was working in a sewing factory quite close to Sumandeep's school. She convinced Mohinder to work in that factory rather than being by herself at home. Mohinder agreed and started working. During the coffee breaks, Mohinder's favorite drink was hot chicken soup from the vending machine. The job lasted a few months, as winter was quite bleak and driving was difficult in the snow and ice. One morning traffic was so slow that our car's gas line froze and it was towed to a garage.

We recovered our 120.0 dollars which we paid for our first accident. One evening when we were visiting a friend and our car was parked on the street, a van sled on the ice and hit our car's bumper and the damage was about 120 dollars. The driver of the van paid us. Our car drove fine and the damage was not bad so we did not get it fixed.

The rough draft of the dissertation was ready to be typed in January, 1966. I got it typed and gave it to Dr. Evans for approval. It was accepted with some suggestions and recommendations for improvements. I was still not quite sure about a specific factor which signaled the cricket to lay overwintering eggs. It was a very important point in the thesis.

One night, I had a dream that it was the difference in day and night temperature. I got up and checked my outside temperature recording charts. The dream was right. I was so excited that I woke up Mohinder and said, "I got the factor." She said, "What factor?" I told her about my dream, the factor and showed her the charts. She said that was it. She was so nice about all this, in the middle of the night. I called Dr. Evans at around 6 AM and gave him the news. He invited me to have breakfast with him. At breakfast we discussed the temperature factor. Dr. Evans commented, "Darshan, put it in your thesis and you are ready for your final exam."

Thus the most important finding in my thesis was a unique adaptation of the cricket to the winter of the Edmonton region. The cricket laid overwintering eggs when the temperature at night was cooler by 20 or more degrees Fahrenheit than the day temperature. It gave the signal to the insect that winter was setting in. Dr. Evans and I agreed on the final exam to defend the dissertation in April, 1966. My external examiner was Dr. N.S. Church from the University of Saskatchewan.

Final Ph.D. Exam

The final exam was an oral exam with a committee of five examiners. On the exam day, after the morning routine, including shower and prayer, I had a light breakfast. While reciting prayer, I reached the University and headed to the exam room. I greeted the examiners with "Good Morning" and they responded back. Dr. Evans introduced

Dr. Church to me as the external examiner. After shaking Dr. Church's hand, I took my seat and the exam started with appropriate questions, such as severe winter conditions and adaptation mechanism of the cricket which was also found in warmer regions. My answer was already explained in the dissertation as the difference in day and night temperature in the fall months.

All went quite well, and after about two hours the exam was over and Dr. Evans asked me to wait outside for the committee to discuss the result. In about ten minutes, Dr. Evans asked me to come in. I was congratulated by the committee, especially by Dr. Church, and was addressed as Dr. Sarai. It was a great moment in my life, and I thanked God for his blessings.

I called Mohinder and Mom and gave them the good news. In the evening, Dr. Church, Mohinder and I were invited to a dinner in the faculty club by Drs. Hocking and Evans who arranged it in my honor. They told me that I had completed the doctoral study in the shortest time, less than three years when normally it took four to five years.

The dinner was quite a treat for both of us. I felt very good about the whole thing and thanked both Drs. Hocking and Evans for their help and for providing me the opportunity to study in their department, and for having Dr. Church as my external examiner. I could not believe that I was Dr. Sarai from then on. I thanked Mohinder and said, "Mohinder, we did it." She gave me a sweet smile in return. Furthermore, I was thinking about my parents and their dream being fulfilled. They would have been so excited to know about it.

Chapter 7
KELOWNA, BRITISH COLUMBIA, CANADA

When I was cleaning and vacating my office at the University of Alberta, Dr. Evans approached me and offered me a job in British Columbia - the Department of Agriculture in the section of Fruit Insect Control. He explained that the job was a summer job in the Okanagan Valley with my station in Kelowna, B. C. He told me that Kelowna was a beautiful town on the Okanagan Lake, and said I deserved a break and some sightseeing after all my hard work. I talked to Mohinder and we were excited to see a little more of Canada before going back to India. Thus we were ready to travel and do some sightseeing.

I was supposed to start the job in May, 1966, before the start of the fruit growing season. We did not have much time to pack and move to Kelowna. However, packing was easy as we gave away some of our things to friends and sold our TV to a student from Panjab. We packed our belongings in the car. Our friends treated us to farewell parties and Mom in particular invited us for dinner an evening before we left for Kelowna. I mentioned with tearful eyes to Mom that we would miss her. She hugged us and said, "You will find new friends wherever you will go, because you are such a lovely family. You will be alright; go and make new friends while exploring some more of Canada." Those were very encouraging words. We left Edmonton with quite an emotional farewell from our friends.

We drove through Calgary, on the Cross Canada Highway #1 and passed through Banff, Lake Louise and stayed overnight in a motel in a small town named Golden. The next morning, we had a nice breakfast and started driving again around 10 AM. We passed through Roger's Pass, a beautiful memorial on top of the breathtaking snow-covered Rockies. Then there were ice fields around the highway in the Glacier National Park.

Roger's pass, with Sumandeep.

We stopped for the scenic views, took pictures, made a few stops for gas and lunch and entered British Columbia (BC). The weather was warmer than Edmonton. We reached Vernon, BC in the afternoon and reported for the job to my supervisor, Mr. Jack Arrand, a horticulturist, in the extension office, BC Department of Agriculture. He wanted me to call him Jack.

My Job

Jack was friendly and easy to get along with. After some paper work and formalities, Jack explained my job responsibilities.

I was to work with a team of Entomologists, Horticulturists, and Plant Pathologists helping fruit growers in the Okanagan and Similkameen valleys, the fruit growing area of British Columbia. My main job was to help in the control of Peach Twig Borer and Cherry Fruit Fly, two major fruit pests in the region. Jack took us to Kelowna. With his help we rented a motel for a week. The next day he took me to my office in Kelowna. It was right on the Okanagan Lake. I shared the office of John Mosey, a plant pathologist. All the staff in the extension department was a friendly and helpful team. After that we went to the Summerland Research Station, only a few miles from Kelowna on the Okanagan Lake. There I met the Research Director, Dr. Harold Madsen (formerly a Professor at the University of California, Berkley). Dr. Madsen gave me a tour of the Research Station, showed me the fruit orchards, and introduced me to his research staff. Some of the latest research was going on in the fruit insect control field at Summerland, such as using the female pheromones (sex hormones) in the traps to attract the male codling moths for females to produce sterile eggs, thus reducing the pest population. Dr. Madsen was friendly, down to earth and a humorous professional. I felt very good about learning better and more environmentally friendly insect control methods, rather than just using pesticides. I explained to Mohinder my job, and told her about all my coworkers. She was happy to see me so excited.

Within a few days we rented a two-bedroom furnished house, 802 Lawrence Ave. that belonged to a teacher who was transferred. It was close to my work and downtown Kelowna. It had a big shady Bing cherry tree, in the fenced backyard, which was loaded with fruit. The front yard was a grassy lawn with an elm tree. It was a nice house for us, and a good place for Sumandeep to play.

We moved into the house and within a few days, two local Panjabi families came to visit us. They invited us for dinner. They came from Panjab and had been settled in Canada for about fifty years. They had large farms and were well known in the town, especially the Basran family. The Basrans were farmers and cattle breeders. Another Panjabi family owned a furniture store in town. They all were friendly people. The Sarai family was a welcome addition to the group. Ladies often got together for tea and shopping, etc. Our neighbors were quite helping and friendly as well. Furthermore, I was home for lunch and to enjoy a soap opera with Mohinder. We felt quite welcome and comfortable within a short time.

Kelowna had natural beauty with mountains and the beautiful Okanagan Lake. After a few weeks, a beautiful little black and white cat visited our home and Sumandeep befriended her and gave her some milk. The cat adopted us and became our pet. Mohinder loved her too. The cat used to sit on Mohinder's lap whenever Mohinder was sitting on the sofa and watching TV or out in the yard.

Mohinder in the backyard with Tina

Mohinder at a beach

Mohinder at Okanagan Lake

We named her Tina. Sumandeep adored Tina and was very happy. She was our pet until December, 1966 when she was found dead in some neighbor's yard. It was so sad, especially for Sumandeep.

Sumandeep Goes to School

Sumandeep turned six in May, 1966 and was ready to go to school that fall. We visited the elementary school which was on the same street at the end of the block from our home. In August, 1966, Sumandeep went to school. We walked her to school for a few days and then she walked herself. She loved her teacher and was quite popular in her class. In the beginning it was harder for Mohinder than for Sumandeep. Mohinder would wait at the front door steps for Sumandeep to come home.

Sumandeep's First Day of School

After getting settled, I planned my work so the summer would be worthwhile. Being an environmentalist, I became interested in the integrated pest control measure. This required the study of the life history and behavior of each pest to be controlled, so that biological and cultural control measures could be incorporated into the use of pesticides for an effective and environmentally friendly pest control.

We used insect traps for determining the emergence and population density of the pests to coordinate the insecticide spray schedule for the most effective control. I used to check the traps in the orchards regularly, observed the activity of the pests, and visited with the growers. It was interesting to interact with and educate the growers. They loved to visit and to observe pest activities with me. Some of them would put hand- picked fruit in my car to show their gratitude. As soon as adult pests were found, a bulletin on the radio was announced stating the designated time, the appropriate insecticide and its dose and spray date.

Many times I would take the family with me to show insect traps and to have an outing and picnic on the lake, since most of the orchards were around the Okanagan Lake. Thus Mohinder and Sumandeep knew about my work.

On special evenings, the Northern Lights created an awesome spectacle. Once we were invited to a barbeque dinner by Dr. Madsen, who lived on the lake close to Summerland. We met his family and enjoyed the hospitality. Mrs. Madsen took pleasure in meeting Mohinder and Sumandeep. After dinner we saw the Northern Lights, called the Aurora Borealis. Mohinder in particular was amazed to see this phenomenon of nature with different colors of lights in the sky. It was a great experience.

So far as my work was concerned, the Peach Twig Borer was very active in 1966; therefore, I had interesting and thorough observations on its life cycle. For preparation to present my research work, Mohinder was my first audience and helper. When I presented a paper in one of the regional meetings of the Entomological Society of British Columbia, Dr. Madsen asked me to publish the study. The study was published, the same year, as a research paper in the Journal of Entomological Society of British Columbia.

The Cherry Fruit Fly was not very active in 1966. I found only two flies in one of the traps and the spray alert was announced on the radio. After the first spray, I did not find any flies, eggs or larvae. Therefore, I was convinced there was no need to spray the orchards any more. As a result, there was a substantial savings for the growers. There was a bumper crop of cherries that year. Growers were happy and I was more confident in the integrated pest management method. It all worked out very well in the end. Growers were educated to use cultural practices like tilling the ground in the orchards in late fall and early spring to expose cherry fruit fly pupae to weather and predators, and to check traps for pest emergence to determine the spray application time. I had a very gratifying experience during the summer of 1966. It was all possible with the team work of the family.

We had great time in Kelowna, Vernon and Penticton, three main cities on Lake Okanagan, with picnics on the lake and enjoying the beautiful beaches. Lake Kalamalka is just east of Okanagan Lake between Vernon and Kelowna. It has many beautiful and different shades of cyan to indigo colors in its depths. It is so scenic to look at. We enjoyed the view.

At Kalamalka Lake

In Kelowna itself, there were so many activities such as high speed boat races, water sports and festivities in the city park right on Okanagan Lake. There was an Ogopogo sculpture in the city park. Ogopogo is a dragon like lake-monster. City Park was within walking distance from our house and we often went there for our evening walks. Kelowna is a beautiful city with lots of things to do and enjoy. We had a great time in Kelowna.

I remember one interesting event when Mohinder received a letter from her dad about the marriage date of sister Malvinder. Mohinder got a little sad that she could not attend the wedding and help Dar Ji. When I tried to share her feelings. Mohinder said, "I wish I was a boy to help my Dar Ji." I said that you would have been a very handsome young man. She smiled and I suggested, "How about seeing you dressed up like a young man." She agreed and dressed up in my clothes with turban. When she looked in the mirror at a very handsome young man, Mohinder Singh, she giggled. Sumandeep could not believe her mama as a dad. It was a laugh of the day for the family.

As Mohinder Singh

As Mohinder Kaur

Our Second Child Came

In the meantime, Mohinder was expecting our second child. We were worried about this pregnancy as we did not have the help we had for Sumandeep's birth. A secretary, Ann Woods, from the extension office, became our personal friend and offered to help Mohinder with the house work and baby care until Mohinder could handle it herself. Our Panjabi friends also assured us of their help. Mrs. Basran loved us so much that she was treating us as her own children. She frequently visited to check in on Mohinder. We were feeling quite comfortable with the situation. She also suggested a good Doctor for Mohinder for regular checkups close to the delivery. It all worked out so very well. Our strong faith in God worked, as always.

We were blessed with the birth of our second child, a daughter, on December 28, 1966. We named her Bina. She was an adorable child with a full crown of black long hair. In the hospital, the nurses nicknamed her as Ringo's (Ringo, one of the English singers, from the Beatles) girlfriend. The hospital where Bina was born was a neat hospital located on Lake Okanagan, with a breathtaking view of the lake and mountains from the window. We were told that delivery in Canada was quite expensive. Lucky for us, there was a law in BC that anyone who lived in BC for four or more months would be medically covered. We had lived in BC for over six months before Bina's birth; therefore delivery, Mohinder, and Bina were medically covered. Sumandeep was so happy to have Bina. She said that her wish for a baby sister had come true. Sumandeep was always there to help us in taking care of Bina. We were so thankful to God for all of this.

Our doctor told us that Mohinder and the baby would have to stay in the hospital for at least a week after the delivery because there was no female adult at our home to take care of them. After a week, Mohinder and Bina came home. Ann Woods bought a beautiful pink baby basket with ribbons and toys for Bina. A nurse from the hospital came daily for about a month to check on Mohinder and baby, and to bathe Bina. Furthermore, Ann was a regular help. Mrs.

Basran was also visiting us regularly. All worked out to great satisfaction.

A Job in America

In October, 1966, I saw an ad in the journal of the Entomological Society of America. This was a job opening in Missouri, USA, for an entomologist, with the Missouri Department of Higher Education, to work on fruit insect pests. I applied for the job and within a month or so, I got a letter from Dr. Kenneth Hanson, Director, Fruit Experiment Station, Mountain Grove, Missouri, showing interest in hiring me. After some communication through writing and telephone calls, he offered me the job. The job required a permanent resident visa of the USA, as the job was permanent with the state of Missouri.

Dr. Hanson wanted me to join them as soon as possible, preferably before the start of the fruit growing season of 1967. He told me that we would soon be informed by the Immigration Department regarding our visas and would get our visas within a month or so.

Moving to United States of America

In January, 1967, we got a letter from the American immigration office in Vancouver, for an interview, implying that our immigrant visas were ready for us to travel to the USA unless there was a medical problem. After consulting our doctor and considering the situation we started packing and getting ready to leave for America.

We put an ad in the newspaper to sell our car. Quite a few people responded and came to look and drive our old Chevy. One of the drivers got the transmission stuck in the third gear, so we were stuck with the car. Luckily, Mrs. Basran and her son, Joginder Singh, came to say goodbye. They saw the car ad in the newspaper. She asked me to sell the car to her. I told her that the transmission was stuck in the third gear. Joginder Singh said, "No problem, I will get it fixed." He asked me the price. I told him that I would sell it for a hundred and fifty dollars which he gave me in cash. Mohinder wanted me to just give them the car for free.

I too felt bad that I was selling an old car stuck in the third gear to a friend for that price. Therefore, I gave back the money. He insisted that I should keep the money and the car was worth it. Then we settled for a hundred twenty dollars. We both felt good. I smilingly asked Mrs. Basran what she would do with our old car. She said, "We will drive it until it works and after that we will park it close to the entry gate of our house in your memory." It was so sweet of her. I almost cried.

On February 25, 1967, we flew from Kelowna to Vancouver. All our friends came to the airport to see us off. Mrs. Basarn hugged us, kissed the children and said with tears in her eyes, "We will miss you all very much; however, we wish that you will be happy in America." The flight was less than an hour long. We stayed overnight in Vancouver, visited the historic Vancouver Gurdwara Sahib, built by early settlers from Panjab. We also visited Chinatown and Stanley Park that afternoon. The next day we went to the US embassy, had our interviews, the physical exams, and got our immigrant visas. We did some more sightseeing that evening and were ready to fly to America. The next morning we flew from Vancouver to Springfield, Missouri.

Chapter 8

MOUNTAIN GROVE, MISSOURI, USA

In Springfield, Missouri, we were received at the airport by Dr. Kenneth Hanson, Director of the Missouri State Fruit Experiment Station. He drove us to Mountain Grove, a small town in Southwestern Missouri, about sixty miles east of Springfield. He offered for us to stay with his family until we found a house for rent. Dr. Hanson was living in the residential quarters at the Fruit Experiment Station, and the guest quarters would be where we stayed.

The next day, he showed me my office, introduced me to the horticulturist, Richard Gainor; Secretary, Camille Archer; the field crew, and took me around the orchards. After that he took my family to downtown Mountain Grove. It was a small town, with a population of about 3,000, and the town square had most of the shops. Everything was within about a five-mile radius. The closest main city for shopping was Springfield.

Within a week we bought a used car, a light blue Ford Galaxy, and opened an account at the bank and started a new life in the USA. Dr. Hanson had already informed the town about us through an article in the local newspaper with my picture. Mountain Grove being a small town, so people already knew about us. Soon I was invited by Dr. Hanson to give a talk at the Rotary Club (the only active civic club in town) about India. It went very well. I became a member of the club soon after that. Sumandeep went to school and became quite popular in her class.

In Mountain Grove we made quite a few friends through my job, by being a member of the Rotary Club, and by Mohinder's being active in the Parent Teachers Association (PTA), a very busy group. We had three families as very close friends: Mackys, McClanahans, and Genericks.

We rented a two bedroom house close to Sumandeep's school. She used to walk to school. I started teaching Mohinder how to drive. I would take her for driving lessons after dinner around the blocks in a new neighborhood close to our home. Within two months she was driving quite confidently. She took the exam and passed both written and driving tests at the same time. She was so proud of herself for being independent to drive around to attend meetings, shopping and visiting friends.

Enjoying back yard spring bloom

With Bina and Sumandeep

Within a few months we rented a much better two-bedroom home with a large dining room, living room, big kitchen, car port and a beautiful yard. It was a country house just outside the main town on the west side. It was fully furnished with nice furniture. Our neighbors were helping and friendly. We were quite happy and comfortable.

We started enjoying the beautiful Ozark Mountains, parks and close- by lakes such as Bull Shoals Lake, Beaver Lake and Table Rock Lake by having picnics and family fun. Theodosia, a beautiful resort and marina on Bull Shoals Lake was one of our favorite choices for a weekend vacation. It was only an hour long drive from Mountain Grove. Another place was Eureka Springs close to Beaver Lake. It has a gorgeous big blue spring. The town is historical with beautiful homes, shops and shows. Popularly it is called "The little Switzerland of USA". Close to Eureka Springs there is a 65.5 ft. high sculpture, the Christ of the Ozarks. All this was only a two-hour drive from Mountain Grove and a great place for long weekends.

My Job

My new position, which started on March 1, 1967, came with the responsibility to study all the diseases and Insect pests of fruit trees and to recommend the appropriate time to spray an effective pesticide for each of them. To have a better understanding of the pests, I met with the Missouri State extension staff and experts from the University of Missouri, Columbia including horticulturists, plant pathologists, and entomologists. Most of them were friendly and helpful.

I prepared myself to practice integrated pest control measures without losing any fruit crops to the pests. The Fruit Experiment Station had large peach, plum, prune, and apple orchards. Furthermore, there were several vineyards of different grape varieties, small patches of strawberries, raspberries, and blueberries. The total orchard area was more than 100 acres.

There was a great concern regarding the grape root borer, a serious and devastating Insect pest of grape vines. This insect is a clear wing moth, resembling a wasp. The larvae of the moth fed on grape roots and ultimately, in the middle of summer, killed the infested vines. Larvae were well protected under the root bark from pesticides and natural enemies. Therefore, they were hard to kill. The control of the grape root borer became my major research project.

In November 1967, I was to attend the annual meeting of the Entomological Society of America in New York City. I asked Mohinder to come with me to enjoy New York City. She agreed and we started planning. Our friend, Bobby McClannahan said that she would take care of Sumandeep and Bina while we were gone. We planned a fun time in New York with stops, such as visiting the Statue of Liberty, Empire State Building, Times Square and

Broadway in the evenings after the meeting. Furthermore, there was a program for wives during the meeting hours to keep them busy and entertained. The conference was in a hotel downtown. During the meeting Mohinder made some friends and met some ladies from the University of Alberta and British Columbia. They went shopping and went to different places on the subway. They even went to a Broadway show. Mohinder was very happy. In the evenings we would go out together to various sites in the fun city and enjoy dinner in some good Indian restaurants. We had a great time on the trip and came back to find Sumandeep and Bina happy being taken good care of by Bobby. They enjoyed the company of Bobby's children, Glenda (daughter) and Clay (son). Clay was Sumandeep's classmate.

While my work was progressing well, we were expecting our third child. All our friends were excited and happy with the news, especially Bobby. Bobby said, "Don't worry, Mohinder, I will help you with the delivery and the baby until you can handle it yourself." It gave us peace of mind and a great encouraging feeling.

Third Child

On April 17, 1968, we were blessed with our third child, a daughter. We named her Nina. Thus we had three international daughters: One from India, one from Canada, and one from the USA. Nina was a very good baby with a smiling face most of the time. She was born in a small hospital in a little town called Houston, in Texas County, Missouri. Sumandeep and Bina were so happy to have her. Our doctor was an interesting well-to-do young physician. He had a helicopter to fly from Mountain Grove to nearby hospitals. All went fine concerning the delivery.

Bobby visited Mohinder in the hospital and adored Nina. She assured Mohinder that all would be all right. She used to come to our home every day after sending her children to school. She would help Mohinder with all the chores, such as preparing breakfast and lunch, bathing Nina, and general housekeeping. She used to leave our home in the afternoon before her children came back from school. This routine worked for a month or so until we could handle the situation. Bobby and Mohinder were like sisters and best friends.

One day, I thanked Bobby for her generous help and asked her how we could pay her back for the help. She smiled and said, "You pay me back by helping someone who needs help." I was overwhelmed to hear that. Bobby was just a wonderful person and we were lucky to have her as a friend. With the grace of God everything worked out very well.

In 1967-68, I studied, in detail, the life history and behavior of different life stages of the grape root borer and came up with an effective cultural control measure: just bury the adults when they emerge from pupae. During my study, it was observed that eggs were laid around the base of the vine. After hatching, tiny larvae burrowed through the soil, reached the roots and fed their way toward the stock (where the trunk and the roots meet) while growing to full size. Then they pupated close to the surface while still being covered with the bark.

Before my study, the recommendations were to expose the base of the vine by removing the soil away from it to expose the pupae to predators. It was not effective because pupae were protected by the bark and adults emerged freely into the atmosphere.

I observed from the lab studies that adults could not emerge from under the soil; even a few inches of soil cover would not let them come out. I recommended forming a ridge about seven inches high around the base of the vines to effectively kill the adults. It turned out to be a very effective cultural practice. I submitted a paper for the annual meeting of the Entomological Society of America. It was accepted. For preparation to present the paper, Mohinder and Sumandeep helped me by listening and making suggestions. It was amazing to know how much they knew about this research.

I published two papers, on the grape root borer, in the Journal of Entomological Society of America. Two more papers on fruit pests, oriental fruit moth and plum curculio, were published in the same journal as well.

Working at the Fruit Experiment Station was quite rewarding with four publications in the Journal of the Entomological Society of America, one of the best known international publications. However, Dr. Hanson and I had a difference of opinion regarding pest management. He believed in the use of pesticides as the only sure control measure for pest control, and I strongly suggested the integrated control measure.

Asthma

While working as an Entomologist, I developed asthma symptoms due to exposure to pesticides by just walking through the orchards for my observations. When I visited my doctor he concluded the exposure to pesticides could be the cause of the problem. I decided that I should get out of the pesticide field as soon as possible. Mohinder agreed with me. She said, "Your health is more important than this job."

Resignation and Trip to India

In Feb 1969, after finishing my research projects and publishing most of my research work, I resigned my job at Missouri State. The job market at that time was bad due to America's involvement in the Vietnam War. Before looking for a job, we planned a trip to India to visit all the relatives after six years of being in North America.

Job Hunting

We came back from India to Mountain Grove and in June 1969, we moved to Mount Vernon, Missouri, where one of our best friends, Dr. Devinder Verma, was a physician in a state hospital. We met the Vermas while in Mountain Grove by chance. They were driving back from St. Louis in a severe snow storm which forced them to stop and stay with us in Mountain Grove. They came to know about us from a gas station. They stayed with us for a couple of days until the roads were clear. Mrs. Veena Verma became a friend of Mohinder immediately and started helping Mohinder in the kitchen and with other house work. After that we became very good friends.

In Mount Vernon, we rented a two bedroom apartment. Mohinder's behavior under this stressful situation was very supportive and encouraging. Smilingly she said, "Don't worry, I will work and you take care of the children while I am at work. Have faith in God and things will work out." She was so inspiring and realistic. Mohinder found a job in a sewing factory, and I started applying at different places for research and teaching jobs. We made some close friends, who helped to make our life in Mount Vernon easy and comfortable.

In September, 1969, one of our friends, Jack Turner, who believed like me in positive thinking and had strong faith in God, planned a job hunting trip. One morning we started out after holding hands and saying a prayer for God's blessing to make our trip a success. We thought that a good job for an entomologist would be either teaching, or working for a plant nursery or similar type of company. The closest town with both these opportunities was Neosho, Missouri, only about fifteen miles from Mount Vernon. We were in

Neosho before noon; we went to the Neosho Nursery and met the manager. He was impressed with my qualifications and readiness to work in any capacity. He was hiring people for landscaping. He said, " We will hire you; however, you should try for a teaching job at Crowder College, a junior Community College and the only college in Neosho." We visited Crowder College and met with the president, Dr. Reed, but he did not have any openings.

He suggested we visit the Water and Wastewater Technical School which was only a few blocks from the college. We thanked him and went to the Water and Wastewater Technical School, and talked to the secretary. She told us that there was an opening in the Environmental Sciences Division; however, the President, Mr. Robert Wright, was in a board meeting. She took my resume and gave it to him. To my surprise, Mr. Wright came out and interviewed me, then consulted with the board. He offered me the job of teaching chemistry and microbiology. The pay was a little higher than the Missouri State job. He wanted me to join as soon as possible. We could not believe that our prayers were answered and I had a teaching job in the environmental field. By this time it was lunch time and we were hungry. We went to the best restaurant in Neosho, named "Crows" and enjoyed lunch. We planned to surprise Mohinder by not showing any excitement right away, after getting back.

When we reached home, Mohinder was waiting to know about the outcome of the job hunting trip. She guessed from my face that nothing had happened. I said calmly, "Well I got a teaching job in a technical school." She said, "You are kidding." Then Jack said that really Darshan had a job offer and could join as soon as possible. We were in a mood for celebrating. We thanked God for the breakthrough and were so excited to move to Neosho.

Chapter 9
NEOSHO, MISSOURI

I joined the Water and Wastewater Technical School and asked the secretary about housing. She gave me the local newspaper which had listed a few houses for rent. I looked over the town.

Neosho

It was a beautiful small town with 8,000 population and town square with county offices in the center, two banks and most of the shops around it. It had roads with gentle sloping hills, a small hospital and other facilities. It was awarded the Flower Box City award of America. I went to the bank and inquired about opening an account. The vice president of the bank was a friendly person who showed special interest in me.

He told me that during the Second World War, he was a prisoner of war in Germany and his roommate was a Sikh gentleman from India who was a great guy and a wonderful friend. Thus the Vice President became my friend. I opened an account and he made a few phone calls regarding a house for us. We were able to find a house outside Neosho on a small farm. He set up an appointment to see the house with the landlady, Mrs. Faye Skelton. The same weekend the whole family came to Neosho and looked at the house. Mrs. Skelton was exceptionally friendly and courteous to us. Our children loved her and played with her dogs when we were going through the house. The whole Skelton family, Mr. Glen Skelton, their daughter Nancy and son Alan, were all very friendly.

We liked the house and the rent was reasonable as well. With the help of our friend, Dr. Verma, we moved from Mount Vernon to Neosho the same weekend. There were two houses on the top of the hill: The landlord's and ours. The houses were quite close with a common big yard and a pond the size of a little swimming pool. There were horses and a pony for the children to ride. Sumandeep went to school in Neosho and rode the school bus along with Nancy. Very soon, the ladies, from the Neosho Welcome Wagon Club with all kind of gifts from the local businesses, visited us. Before long, we were feeling quite at home in Neosho.

Within a few weeks, we went to Springfield to buy a new car. We bought a 1969 Ford Torino Station wagon, a beautiful tan colored car with dark brown trim and blue interior. The trunk of the car could be converted into two seats or a flat bed. Mohinder and the children loved the car and we were excited to make some long road trips to see more of the United States of America. Mohinder made a Styrofoam mattress with a beautiful flowery cover for the children to play and to sleep on while on long trips. Soon after that we bought a second car, a used Volkswagen, for me. Thus Mohinder had the station wagon when I was at work.

Got a Pet

Skelton farm was a dumping ground for unwanted pets. People would dump them close to the farm and pets would walk to the Skelton barn and house. A tabby yellow cat with a half cut off tail showed up at our house. The children gave him milk. He became a regular visitor and the children liked him and wanted him as their pet. Mohinder and I were slowly convinced that it was OK. I made the deal with the children that the cat should stay out at night. They agreed and we named the cat "Duke" who turned out to be a very lovable pet. He played with the children, never scratched anyone or anything, never made any mess in the house, walked the children to the bus stop, and walked with us, like a dog, on our evening walks.

After a six month probation period, I got my first raise and confirmation. To my surprise, the president of the school offered me the position of the Chairman of the Environmental Sciences Division. I felt honored and accepted it. Things were progressing well in Neosho and we were ready to buy a house by saving some money for the down payment.

Bought a Home

We bought our first three bedroom home in town in 1971. We got a very good deal on the house, rather than making a down payment, the Mortgage Company gave us some money to furnish the house as the house was appraised for more than the selling price. Using this money and some of our savings, we got new carpeting, bought new furniture, a color TV (quite expensive then) and new appliances. Mohinder made beautiful drapes for the living room picture window and curtains for all the other rooms. Then house became beautiful and comfortable before we even moved in. We put a swing set in the backyard for the children to play.

Our home was on top of the hill on Beverly Street in a good and friendly neighborhood. There was an elderly couple, the Crews, next door to us. They loved our children. We had a large backyard extending all the way to the woods. All backyards on our side of the street were without fences so children could play freely. The house was only a five minute drive from my work.

To stay in touch with Indian friends, we found one Sikh family, Dr. Kirpal Singh's, in Nevada, Missouri, about sixty miles from Neosho on the way to Kansas City. They had three children. One of their daughters was about the same age as Sumandeep. Dr. Verma's family often visited us as well.

We got a toy black French poodle pup and named him "Jojo." Duke and Jojo became good friends. Duke never did mind any other pets or children in the house. Jojo was only about six months old when he got run over by a car and died. It was so sad. Duke, after being our pet for five years, got sick. He was diagnosed by the veterinarian with some mysterious old age disease. After a few months of being sick, Duke just disappeared and never came back. We missed him a lot and looked for him everywhere.

After hanging the last curtain in the house.

After losing Duke, the children wanted to have another cat or dog. One day we went to Joplin, Missouri, a bigger town and only about ten miles from Neosho. There, we visited the humane society's animal shelter where we saw a cute miniature schnauzer dog, named Schnuffs. The children played with him and liked him. We brought him home after getting him checked by a veterinarian. He loved the children and soon became a good pet.

During that time, Mohinder joined ladies' clubs and was well known in town. She was active in the ladies' bridge club, the bowling league, gourmet club and ladies' Literary Club of which she became the president later. Due to her being very active in the community she was in the newspaper a few times.

The Gourmet Club gave an international touch to Mohinder's cooking skills. She used to prepare some delicious Mexican dishes like Spanish chicken and Rice Sabrosa; Italian dishes such as lasagna, various noodle casseroles and Spaghetti; others like pig in the blanket (hotdog rolled in a bun) and various desserts. I used to come home for lunch to enjoy her home cooking.

Once a year husbands were invited by the Gourmet Club to a progressive dinner starting at 5 PM and ending around 10 PM. In the first house we had appetizers and drinks, in the second home there was the main course meal and in the third house the desserts and coffee. This event was so popular that we would wait anxiously for the next year's dinner.

Dr. Ronald Layton (Ron), the president of the Water and Wastewater Technical School became a good friend of mine and his wife Judy became a friend to Mohinder. They both belonged to the same ladies' groups. The Laytons had one child, a daughter, Suzanne, who was a playmate of our children. Thus we became quite close family friends.

Brother Jarnail Singh Came

During this time my brother Jarnail Singh who told me in Delhi, "Brother I will follow you." came to America in 1969 as an immigrant under the professional quota system. When we received him in Springfield, Missouri, he hugged me and said, "I told you that I will follow you soon." It was a great feeling to have a brother in USA. After a few weeks in Neosho, he moved to Houston, Texas, where he had some relatives from his in-law's side. We made our first long trip in the station wagon to Houston to celebrate Christmas of 1969 with him. We had a great time in Houston and did lots of sightseeing such as the Space Center and Galveston to mention a few.

He moved back to Neosho to receive his family, wife and son, who came from England. Thus there was more fun time with the family like sightseeing in the Ozarks, going to Silver Dollar City and the beaches on Table Rock Lake and more. Jarnail Singh started working at Buddy L., a local grill making factory.

However, he was not happy with the work and pay. In 1970, Jarnail Singh moved to Kansas City which was the largest city close to Neosho, with better job opportunities, there he found a job to his liking. Soon after that his family joined him. In Kansas City he found three Sikh families. We often met them whenever we were in Kansas City. Slowly, we had some social and religious activities, such as celebrating Indian festivals, holidays, and children's birthdays. Soon we knew the Sikh families around Kansas City in the four state region of Missouri, Kansas, Iowa, and Nebraska. There were only about ten Sikh families in the whole region. They were very enthusiastic and dedicated to Sikhism.

Mohinder was a very caring and sharing person. She had a very good system to welcome guests and family members. Making them feel welcome and at home within a short time. She used to plan ahead for meals, sleeping and other necessary requirements, including fun activities at the nearby attractions, parks and rivers. She would be so intimate with the guests that in a short time they felt as they were part of the family and our home was like theirs.

Ladies would help prepare meals. The children would play with Sumandeep, Bina and Nina and had fun with our pets.

Midwest Sikh Association

One day in 1970, we visited Kansas City to celebrate my nephew's birthday. Besides us, there were two other Sikh families attending the celebration. While celebrating the birthday we came up with the idea of forming a Sikh Association in Kansas City. It was a noble idea. We agreed to call it the Midwest Sikh Association (MSA). We collected ten dollars per family to start the organization. Everybody was so happy and started dreaming about having a Gurdwara Sahib (Sikh temple) in the Kansas City area.

After that we started having monthly congregations, rotating among families within the four state region. These meetings were popularly known as "Sat Sangs" which meant true religious congregations. These services included recital from Sri Guru Granth Sahib Ji, singing hymns, telling Sikh history stories, Karah Parshad and Langar (religious vegetarian meal).

The emphasis was mainly on the children's participation. The children's program was one of the most important parts of the Sat Sang to teach them Sikh values to live a happy, healthy and successful life in America. They used to participate in Kirtan (singing the hymns from Sri Guru Granth Sahib). There used to be competitions on special occasions in Sakhis (Sikh history stories) with prizes. Sikh families in the region became like a large family. Ladies prepared the Langar.

The host family assigned some of the langar items such as chapattis, dal, vegetables and raita (home- made yogurt with diced or grated cucumbers, etc.) to participating families. This would make it easier for the host family to serve a large group of participants. These meetings were very rewarding and satisfying for those of us living in America. Our children got more connected with our faith, culture and the Sikh community in the Midwest. The Midwest Sikh Association was getting more organized and publicized. In 1973, we wrote by-laws for the MSA and got it registered as a nonprofit religious and cultural organization.

Brother Pritam Singh Came

In 1970, my elder brother Pritam Singh and his wife, two sons and a daughter, came from England to Neosho, on their way to Ypsilanti, Michigan. There he was selected as an exchange professor from England to the Eastern Michigan University to teach in the Education Department. It was Christmas time and there was so much excitement for the holiday celebration. It was the first time in the USA that we had three brothers and their families together to celebrate Christmas. Mohinder prepared a traditional Christmas dinner with baked turkey, stuffing, mashed potatoes with gravy, cranberry sauce and pumpkin pie. We had a fully decorated Christmas tree with gifts under it. The children were so anxious to open their gifts. It was lots of fun. Bina's 4th birthday celebration on Dec. 28, 1970 was a kind of extended holiday celebration. It was quite a memorable time for the Sarai family.

During the summer of 1971, we made our second long trip. This time we drove to Ypsilanti, Michigan, to visit Brother Pritam Singh. By now, we were a well-organized team for the long trips. We had an atlas to figure out our route. I would have the route written on a piece of paper with Mohinder as a navigator; we had our overnight stay decided and possible sightseeing on the way. We used a cassette player with Gurbani tapes to listen while driving. We had a cooler with drinks and sandwiches, etc. I used to be the main driver and Mohinder drove as needed. Mohinder and

Sumandeep decided the restaurants to stop for gas and eating on the way. Bina and Nina had their pillows, coloring books and other items to keep them busy and comfortable while travelling. It was a great team effort to travel. We reached Ypsilanti on the second day.

We spent a week with Brother Pritam Singh and visited Detroit and various attractions around it such as the Henry Ford Museum in Dearborn, and downtown Detroit. One day we took a trip to the Michigan State University campus in East Lansing. I was particularly interested to see the Agriculture Research Station. Our children had a chance to enjoy themselves and interact socially during that time. It was a great trip.

After that we made several long driving trips: to Washington, DC; to Miami Beach Florida, Everglades and Cypress Gardens; to Detroit, Toronto and Niagara falls; to Chicago and Springfield, Illinois and more for yearly family summer vacations.

Our children were doing well in the Neosho School System and their extracurricular activities. Sumandeep was a member of the Pep Club and local Four H club. Bina and Nina were members of Girl Scouts and the Softball league. Mohinder was making sure that they were growing up the best possible way to be happy, healthy and successful. For the proper dress up for special occasions, Mohinder would sew the appropriate dresses, even prom dress for Sumandeep. Mohinder, being an artist, had a passion for sewing beautiful clothes. During winter knitting sweaters, scarfs and mittens for the family was a great way to enjoy winter.

Sumandeep was one of the top students in her class. She was awarded membership in the National Honors Society. She was interested in going to the University of Missouri Kansas City (UMKC) Medical School. It was a six year comprehensive Doctor of Medicine (MD) program for high school graduates. UMKC was very selective with a limited enrollment. In 1978, Sumandeep was the only graduate from her class to be selected in that program.

Becoming American Citizens

All five of us became American Citizens in 1972, by passing the exam and taking the oath of citizenship. It was a great feeling. It opened the door for some of our immediate relatives to immigrate to the USA.

My younger brother, Karnail Singh, and his family emigrated from England to America in 1973. We were quite excited to see them in America. Karnail Singh is an athlete, always interested in games and particularly running. He used to play badminton with the children in the backyard and acted as their elder brother. His wife had met us for the first time. Mohinder developed quite a close relationship with her in a short time. We went out for sightseeing and boating, etc. They stayed with us for a few months and then moved to Kansas City and settled there. Thus I had both my brothers in Kansas City.

Trip to India

We made our second trip to India in the summer of 1974 to stay in touch with our family members and friends. Our friend, Helen Mackey, from Mountain Grove, came with us. Our first stop was Bombay to visit S. Avtar Singh Arora, Mohinder's maternal uncle, who was living there with his family. Besides enjoying his hospitality, he took us to various attractions such as Gateway of India, Dadar Beach and Kamala Nehru Gardens to mention a few. Mohinder and I went to Sri Hazur Sahib, Nader (close to Bombay) to pay our homage. It is one of holiest Sikh shrines. This is where Sri Guru Govind Singh Sahib, tenth Sikh Guru, installed Sri

Guru Granth Sahib Ji as the eternal Sikh Guru, before bodily departing this world.

After spending a week in Bombay we took a train to Agra to visit S. Bhagwant Singh Arora, Mohinder's eldest maternal uncle, who was settled there. He being quite resourceful and influential, arranged our visit to the Taj Mahal on a full moon night, when the sight of the Taj Mahal is the most beautiful like a white marble dream building in the blue sky. We had a picnic dinner on the lawn and enjoyed the scene. Helen in particular was amazed with this spectacle. It was the highlight of our trip, especially for Helen, who saw the Taj Mahal for the first time. After Agra we went to Delhi. Helen went to Nepal to enjoy the Himalayas. We enjoyed visiting our relatives in Delhi, sightseeing and paying our homage to Sikh Gurwaras. Then we left for Hoshiarpur to spend time with Mohinder's family. We had our 15th wedding anniversary at Hoshiarpur where our relationship began. It was fun to watch Sumandeep, Bina and Nina enjoying the company of Dar Ji and Bhen Ji in particular. It was a memorable family get together after five years. After Hoshiarpur, we went to Amritsar to pay our respect at Sri Harmandir Sahib and visit Jhaiee Ji, Uncle S. Jagjit Singh Arora, sister Malvinder and other relatives. All our relatives were so nice, hospitable and overwhelmed to see our children quite grown and well behaved.

Our children enjoyed the India trip for all that sightseeing and meeting all the relatives especially, Jhaiee Ji, Dar Ji and Bhen Ji. This time, the children were old enough to interact and enjoy their love and company much better than the previous trip.

After we came back from India our other relatives came, either to visit us in Neosho or to get settled in America. Mohinder's cousin Dolly (Rajiv K. Arora- Brara) and her husband visited us for about two weeks. Mohan auntie visited us twice in Neosho. The first time by herself and second time with her husband, S. Rattan Singh Srikureja. After having a great time with auntie and uncle in Neosho, we made a car trip to Toronto, Canada and Niagara Falls. One of their friends from Thailand was settled there. We enjoyed the trip very much.

With Dolly (Rajiv K. Arora-Brara)

Mohinder's brother, Arvinderpal Singh came as an immigrant in 1975. Then Mohinder's sister, Malvinder, and her family immigrated in 1976. Thus we had a large part of our family in the USA. It became fun to celebrate holidays like Thanksgiving, Christmas, the Fourth of July and birthdays with our family members.

Jarnail Singh, being a daring and adventurous person, was very well settled in Kansas City with his own house in Blue Springs, a suburb of Kansas City. Therefore all our relatives, after getting their Social Security Cards, driver's licenses and having their own cars, moved to Kansas City as Jarnail Singh was there to help them find work and get settled. Thus all our relatives were settled in Kansas City and its suburbs.

In the meantime, the Water and Wastewater Technical School started having some financial problems in 1976. We lost the pension plan in 1977 and some other benefits later without any satisfactory explanation from the authorities. I got concerned about my future with the Water and Wastewater Technical School. After Sumandeep was accepted into Medical School, we planned a move to Kansas City. The whole family got excited about the plan. I started looking for a job in the Kansas City area. I applied for an opening as Lab Supervisor, Water District # 1 of Johnson County, Kansas, the second largest water utility in the Kansas City Metropolitan area. I was interviewed by the Superintendent of the plant, Mr. Bennet Kwan, originally from Hong Kong. We had a positive, friendly talk and all looked good; however, the job offer process was going to be slow. He liked me and assured me that I was the best candidate for the job.

Chapter 10
MOVED TO KANSAS CITY, MISSOURI

I resigned my job at the Water and Wastewater Technical School, put our house up for sale, and started looking for a house in the Kansas City area. Within a few months we bought a home in Raytown, Missouri, a suburb of Kansas City. It was close to most of our relatives and the UMKC.

We moved to 9351E. 77th St (a four bedroom brick house), Raytown in August, 1978, just before the start of school. It was a scary situation as we had two homes with mortgage payments and no job. However, we had strong faith in God and felt that we made the right move and things would work out. After a month, we sold our house in Neosho and had a job offer from Water District # 1, Johnson County. In the meantime, Sumandeep started the UMKC medical school and Bina and Nina went to Raytown Elementary School.

Mohinder a Teacher

Remembering Dad's advice, as the children were quite grown by now and in school, Mohinder started looking for a teaching job. Mohinder was hired by the Independence School System as a teacher in the Head Start program. Her job was from 9AM to 2:30 PM. In the morning, she used to get the children ready, gave them breakfast and sent them to school before going to work. In the afternoon she was home before they came from school to give them a snack. Thus Mama was always home for them. She enjoyed the routine and liked her job. My work was from 7:30AM to 3:30PM. I used to arrive home at 4:30PM.

In the evening before dinner, we helped the children with their homework. After dinner we used to go for evening walks, which involved talking with the children about their day at school and studies. For extracurricular activities, Bina and Nina were members of Girl Scouts and were taking dance classes. Although Sumandeep was very busy with her Medical studies, she would still find time for the family, and to play with sisters. Friday was family night when the whole family would go to the movies, shows and dinners, etc. Some of our favorite places were Starlight Theater and Tiffany's Attic dinner playhouse. On Sundays we would have prayer together and understanding the interpretation of Gurbani. During summer, we took vacations at interesting places like Tan-Tar-A resort, Osage Beach and Lake of the Ozarks. Thus life was quite busy, interesting and enjoyable, with children growing under Mama's tender loving care and guidance.

Mohinder's job involved visits to children's homes and age appropriate activities to use at home for parent involvement, writing reports, in addition to her regular teaching. For her class room, she had an assistant. To further her education and improve her teaching skills, she took classes at UMKC in early childhood education, exceptional children, child development, child guidance and child abuse and neglect. She earned an Associate of Child Development Association (CDA). For her teaching, she received some awards from the Independence School System.

All was working out wonderfully well and we were happy being close to our relatives and friends, living in the Kansas City Metropolitan area. We were very active in our Panjabi community with monthly congregations and other social activities. All this made us firm believers of "Trust in God and do right."

Spiritual and Cultural Aspect of Life

Besides our work, we were seriously concerned about the spiritual and cultural aspects of life, especially for our children. We wanted them to grow up with the same values which we had as parents. For that, it was normal for the first generation immigrants from India to be concerned about maintaining their cultural and religious practices. America, as a land of opportunity, was different culturally and had different values, with more freedom for children. We wanted our children to take advantage of the best values of both cultures to be better than us in life. We did not want them to be confused and lost between the two cultures. In our family, to keep them connected with their roots, I used to tell them bed time stories from Sikh history and the importance of faith in life. Also, we used to visit India every five years or so for them to meet relatives and to keep up with our traditions and roots. Furthermore, we continued to have social and religious activities among the Indian and the Sikh families in the Kansas City area.

Finally, in 1978 the MSA was incorporated. By this time the MSA had enough money to start planning a Gurdwara Sahib building in the Kansas City area. In 1981, MSA bought a three acre lot in Shawnee, Kansas, which was zoned for religious buildings. From then on, momentum was set to build a Gurdwara Sahib. There was lots of excitement and devotion for the project. In 1985, a ground breaking ceremony was planned on Sri Guru Nanak Dev Ji's birthday (full moon in October) with Akhand Paath (an uninterrupted, continuous, and complete recitation of Sri Guru Granth Sahib in about 48 hours) followed by Kirtan (devotional singing). Devoted Sikhs and preachers were invited from India, California, and the four state region. It was an exciting occasion. On the ground breaking day, it was very cold and sleeting wintry weather. However, nothing could dampen our enthusiasm. The whole congregation (sangat), after

Akhand Paath, went to the future Gurdwara Sahib site. The ceremony was led by Bhai Jiwan Singh Ji from California. It started with Kirtan of five hymns from Sri Guru Granth Sahib Ji and Ardas (blessing prayer). According to Sikh tradition, we all stood in the sleet with our shoes off and hands folded in prayer before the ground breaking which was five shovel cuts by five Sikhs. It was a very impressive scene of devotion and strong faith. After the ceremony the sangat had Guru Ka Langar at a club house in Shawnee.

In 1988, the Gurdwara Sahib Building was completed, a permit for the use of the building for congregations was obtained, and weekly services were started. Our prayers were answered and our dream was a reality. It is a beautiful brick building with a large parking lot and city- approved landscaping. After that the Sikh community in Kansas City started growing quite rapidly, perhaps due to the attraction of Gurdwara Sahib besides other reasons.

We had a reverend preacher (Granthi/Bhai Sahib), Giani Udham Singh Ji, from Punjab who was newly emigrated from Africa. He resided in the building where he conducted daily services and weekly congregations, taught Panjabi and reading scripture to the children. He also hosted Sikh visitors to the Gurdwara Sahib. The Sikh community was blessed in the region and we were more than happy that our children were learning the Sikh faith and spiritual values to become better Sikhs. Slowly, we became a well-known Sikh community in Shawnee in particular and in the region in general by participating in community activities such as Shawnee Days Parade (an annual city function) by serving free drinks to participants, having blood donations through the Red Cross, and so on.

Our children were growing up with good educations, as part of a big Sarai family (about 32 members including children) which was joined by S. Avtar Singh Arora, Mohinder's maternal uncle and best childhood friend who immigrated with his family in 1983. Christmas, Thanksgiving, and Fourth of July were family reunion celebrations. It was great fun. Children were keeping up with our cultural and religious traditions while growing up in American Culture.

Sumandeep graduated from the UMKC medical school in 1984 and started her internship in St. Louis. Nina was also interested in the UMKC medical school. Considering Nina's grades and other achievements in high school, she was asked through a letter by the Dean of UMKC to apply for admission to the six- year MD program. It was an honor for a high school senior to get such a letter. Nina, being modest, did not make a big deal of the letter from the dean. She applied and was accepted for the UMKC Med School where she started in 1986. Bina, on the other hand, was interested in the liberal arts, especially fine art. She was talented in drawing and paintings. We encouraged her to pursue the career of her choice. She joined a local community college. As their studies were progressing well, we were thinking to move into a better home, possibly closer to my work. In 1989, we found and bought a nice four bedroom home in Olathe, Kansas.

Olathe, Kansas

In March 1989, we moved to our Olathe home, 16620 W132 St, Olathe. A very comfortable home in a very nice neighborhood. It was close to Mohinder's brother, Arvinderpal Singh in Olathe, sister Malvinder and uncle, S. Avtar Singh Arora, both living in Overland Park with their families. Thus, Mohinder had three families from her side quite close by. Furthermore, the home was close to my work; however, Mohinder had to drive a little farther to her job than before which she did not mind. Nina graduated from Medical

School in 1992. Around this time we planned the next phase of our lives to get our daughters married and settled in their lives and professions.

Daughters' Weddings

Sumandeep got married in 1989 to Dr. Mark Groh, a cardiothoracic surgeon, a very bright and down to earth young man. For the marriage ceremony, Sumandeep's maternal grandparents (Dar Ji and Bhen Ji) came from India to participate. Dar Ji and Bhai Udham Singh Ji performed the Anand Karj (wedding ceremony), the Sikh traditional wedding. Dar Ji recited Lavan, marriage hymns, from Sri Guru Granth Sahib Ji and Bhai Udham Singh Ji did the Kirtan part while the couple went around Sri Guru Granth Sahib four times to commit themselves to their married life. It was followed by Guru Ka Langar. All members of our family participated in the ceremony and blessed the couple for a happy and successful married life. After a week there was a garden wedding ceremony in Dallas- Fort Worth, Texas. It was a wonderful feeling for the whole family. Sumandeep was already practicing medicine in a hospital in Dallas- Fort Worth.

At Sumandeep's wedding

In 1990, we went to India for Bina's wedding. She married Harpreet Singh Grover, a computer scientist. Nina got married in 1991 to Sukhdev Singh Srikureja, a computer science graduate with a business major. He was a very promising business man. The marriage took place in Bangkok with a great celebration according to Thai Sikh tradition. Nina's friends from med school and one of her professors participated. Thus we had all our daughters married within three years. After her graduation, Nina moved to Thailand and has been practicing medicine there. To practice in Thailand, she had to take the medical board exam in Thai which she passed. It was an unbelievable achievement for a person who was born, raised and educated in America.

In the meantime, Mohinder's younger sister, Upinder and her family and her younger brother, Harinderpal and his family immigrated in 1991 and 1992, respectively. Thus Mohinder had all her family members in the USA. It was a wonderful family reunion.

Grandchildren

We were blessed with our first grandchild, Esha, Bina's daughter, on Apr. 27, 1991. The whole family was there at her delivery at St. Joseph Hospital, MO. Mohinder was delighted to hold her and rock her. Mohinder was so excited to take care of her, and delighted in bathing her, feeding her and playing with her. She wanted to spend the maximum time with her. Esha brought so much happiness to the family that there was not a dull moment in the house. She made us grandparents, Nanima and Nana Ji, Panjabi terms for maternal grandmother (Nanima) and grandfather (Nana-Ji), respectively.

With Esha

Esha was followed by Benjamin, Sumandeep's son in 1994. The same year Nina had her first daughter, Karuna, in Bangkok. In 1996, Sumandeep had a daughter, Camille, and Nina had a daughter, Anya. In 1999, Nina had a son, Arjun, and Sumandeep had a son, Jay. Mohinder was there as helper at the birth of each of the seven grandchildren. Thus from 1991 through 1999 we were blessed with seven grandchildren, four girls and three boys. Each one of them is very bright and sweet in their own way. They made us feel happy, healthy, and young. We enjoyed every moment when they were around.

One day in 1993 when I came home from work, Mohinder showed me an ad in the Kansas City Star newspaper about a car, black 1993 J30 Infinity, and she showed interest in seeing it. I liked the car as well. The car was almost new, having been driven only a thousand miles. The next day we made the appointment and went to see it.

We bought the car and Mohinder loved it. It was her favorite car from then on.

J30 Infinity

Mohinder got Esha admitted in the Association of Montessori International (AMI), State Line, MO in 1995. AMI was on Mohinder's way to work. After getting herself ready, Mohinder used to get Esha ready, give her breakfast and take her to school. She would pick Esha up on her way back. Mohinder loved to spend this quality time with Esha. Esha on her part loved to go with Nanima to school. At AMI, Esha was quite popular among her classmates and teachers. She participated in the play "Black Birds and Apple pie" and acted as a black bird so well that she stole the show.

By now, Mohinder and I were feeling like retiring and spending more time with our daughters and grandchildren. We wanted to do the things we could not do while working, like more travelling and pursuing our hobbies. Mohinder loved playing tennis and I wanted to focus on writing.

One day, close to the end of March 1997, Mohinder came home from work and said, "I quit my job, because I want to spend more time with the family and play tennis." At that time she was still under contract for the rest of the school year. I said, "Mohinder, what about your contract?" She responded, "I don't care." We were so relieved that she wouldn't have to drive so far. She was so happy to be home. She started playing tennis and having fun with Esha. She had Esha begin tennis lessons at Golds Gym. Thus part of our retirement started in 1997.

Chapter 11
RETIRED LIFE

Mohinder had taken an early retirement from the Independence School System in 1997 after working for over 19 years. After a little over twenty years, I retired from Water District #1 in Feb. 1999. It was planned that after retirement we would go back to India, pay homage and thanks to God by visiting holy Sikh Shrines in India and Pakistan before starting a retired life.

The trip was coordinated with the 300th anniversary of the birth of Khalsa which comes on April 13th, called Vaisakhi. On this day in 1699 Guru Govind Singh Ji, our 10th Guru, Amrittized (baptized) Sikhs, gave them the name Singh as the second part of the name for men and Kaur for ladies. Singh and Kaur mean lion and princess, respectively. Thus he made the Sikhs both saint and soldier at the same time, complete with faith and self-defense. To celebrate 1999 Vaisakhi, people came to Panjab from all over the world to participate.

Trip to the Orient

Within a month of retirement we (Mohinder, Bina, Esha and I) left the USA for Thailand to spend time with Nina. Nina was expecting a son and Mohinder wanted to be there to help Nina and celebrate the birth of our grandson. His arrival was expected close to the middle of March, which gave us enough time to do some sightseeing in Thailand until he was born.

We took a tour of Northern Thailand, including Chaing Mae, Chiang Rai, and the Golden Triangle (notorious for opium growing). The triangle covers Northern Thailand, Eastern Burma, and Western Laos. Thailand,

Laos, and Burma share borders and engage in lots of business in that area. We took a boat across the famous Me Kong River to Laos and did some shopping there. It was an interesting trip.

India and Pakistan

We came back from the trip, and our grandson, Arjun Singh, was born on March 17th, St Patrick's Day. After a week of celebrating Arjun Singh's birth, we flew from Bangkok to Delhi where we visited our relatives and toured historical buildings such as Red Fort and Qutab Minar. We paid homage to Gurdwara Sis Ganj Sahib (site where Guru Teg Bahadur achieved martyrdom by the orders of Mughal Emperor, Aurang Zeb), Gurdwara Bangla Sahib, and Gurdwara Rakab Ganj Sahib. The last two sites are in memory of Guru Harkishan Ji's passing and cremation of Guru Teg Bahadur Ji's body, respectively. These three Gurdwaras are very important Sikh holy shrines in Delhi. The Delhi visit was quite exciting for Esha in particular, because it was her first visit to India.

After a week in Delhi, we went to Agra to show Esha the Taj Mahal and Fatehpur Sikri, once capital of Mughal Emperor Akbar. After that we left for Panjab. We were received by my brother Pritam Singh at Chandigarh, the capital of Panjab. He lives in Panch Kula, a suburb of Chandigarh. After enjoying a memorable stay with my brother's family, we went to Hoshiarpur to spend some time with Mohinder's parents. In Hoshiarpur, I showed Esha Panjab University College where Mohinder and I graduated and the little apartment where I lived as a graduate student. Esha had a great time meeting the family in India and seeing all these places where Mohinder and I had spent part of our young lives. From Hoshiarpur, we went to Amritsar and visited friends and relatives, Harmandir Sahib, and Khalsa

College Amritsar. We saw the house where we lived in Khalsa College. All this was an eye opener for Esha.

From Amritsar, we went to Pakistan to visit holy Sikh shrines there. According to our plans we stayed mainly in Lahore (capital of the Punjab province of Pakistan). From there we visited the holy shrines Nankana Sahib, the birth place of Sri Guru Nanak Dev Ji, founder of Sikhism, and other Gurdwaras close by signifying his childhood. It was an unbelievable spiritual journey for all of us to see these holy places in Pakistan for the first time.

Then we went to see Gurdwara Panja Sahib in Hasan Abdal, where Guru Nanak Dev Ji met a Muslim saint, Wali Quandhari, who had a spring and controlled the water in this arid land. Guru Nanak Dev Ji's companion, Bhai Mardana Ji got thirsty and badly needed a drink of water. Guru Ji sent him three times to Wali Quandhari for a drink of water. At Mardana Ji third trip, Wali Quandhari said, "Go and ask your Guru Nanak to give you a drink of water and don't you ever come back." Bhai Mardana told Guru Nanak about that. Guru Nanak Dev Ji moved a stone close by him with a stick and a spring gushed out with cool and clear water. Guru Nanak Dev Ji asked Bhai Mardana to quench his thirst. This spring was draining Wali Quandhari's water.

While drinking the water, Mardana saw that Wali Quandhari had pushed a boulder from the top of his hill which was rolling down straight toward Guru Nanak Ji. Guru Nanak Dev Ji lifted his arm and stopped the boulder with his hand. The boulder has a permanent hand impression of Guru Nanak Dev Ji. The name Panja Sahib, comes from his hand impression. By seeing all this, Wali Quandhari came down from his hill, visited with Guru Nanak Dev Ji and became his devotee by learning that all resources are a gift from God; we need to share them among us as we are all the children of God. The water from the spring became the origin of a large stream which is the water supply for the city and source of irrigation for land in the region.

We took an early morning bath at the Panja Sahib, had some breakfast and climbed the Wali Quandhari hill. The trail to the hill is quite steep and rough, perhaps the way it was during Guru Nanak Dev Ji's time. Esha still remembers this part of the trip very dearly. It was one of the highlights of our trip to Pakistan and a lesson in the way Guru Nanak Dev Ji taught some of the misguided 'so called' spiritual people.

In Lahore, we visited Gurdwara Dehra Sahib close to the river Ravi. It is at the site where Sri Guru Arjan Dev Ji (5th Sikh Guru) achieved martyrdom by the orders of Mughal Emperor Jahangir. Close to the Gurdwara Sahib, there are other historical buildings about Maharaja Ranjit Singh who ruled the greater Panjab area during the nineteenth century. Lahore was the capital city.

We made slides of our journey and Esha presented a slide show to her class about the trip, the requirement for missing her school. Esha's presentation was so good that her teacher applauded and congratulated Esha for learning so much on her trip. She surprised me with her presentation. The purpose of the whole adventure was well served: we paid thanks for all the blessings by visiting holy shrines, and Esha was further connected to our family and faith by this six week trip.

Asheville, North Carolina

Sumandeep had been living in Biltmore Park, Asheville, North Carolina, since 1995. It is a beautiful, historic, medium sized city, surrounded by mountains, with two small rivers flowing through it, and towering pine trees beautifying its landscape. It is only a four hour drive from beautiful beaches and has all the medical, recreational, and other facilities for retirement.

Sumandeep asked us to move there after retirement to be close to her. We visited her several times and we liked it very much, having milder weather than Kansas City, both in summer and winter. Once Mohinder was visiting Sumandeep and saw new homes just being built in her neighborhood. They both liked a home still under construction, and we could get some changes made to our liking. Mohinder called me and said that she liked a house in Biltmore Park close to Sumandeep's home. When she described the house to me, I said, "Mohinder buy it." So she did. It is a beautiful four bedroom home close to all the facilities and only about a mile from Sumandeep's home at that time. It has a beautiful trail in the back which goes through Biltmore Park for walking, jogging and bike riding. There is a woody area with a very clear spring fed stream which runs along the trail. It was the perfect home for our retired life.

We moved to 1360 Heath brook Cir., Asheville, NC, in May, 2000 and have been enjoying it and the company of Sumandeep and grandchildren ever since.

Mohinder a Tennis Player

Mohinder loved playing tennis so she joined the Asheville Racquet Club which had beautiful tennis courts and other athletic facilities. She joined two tennis teams, playing on Tuesday and Thursday. She was the organizer of the Tuesday team, for which she arranged the players, prepared the schedule and secured the tennis court for weekly playing. Besides her regular playing, if she could substitute for someone she loved to do that. Sumandeep was also her team member. Their mother and daughter team was the best for doubles. Besides playing, the team members were close friends, often going for lunch or coffee after the game.

Nina is a good tennis player as well. Mohinder had Esha join tennis team in high school. Esha too turned out to be a good player and sometimes played as a substitute on the Mohinder's team. Tennis became a favorite sport of the Sarai family. On weekends and during the summer we would go to the Biltmore Park area public tennis courts to hit balls. Mohinder involved me in playing tennis but I was not good at it. She taught me all the rules of the game which made me enjoy watching tennis matches. We watched all the four major tennis events: the Australian Open, French Open, Wimbledon and US Open.

Our daughters sent us in 2009, to the US Open at Ashe Stadium Flushing, New York, as a gift for Mohinder's 70th birthday. She was thrilled with this gift. At the US Open, it was so much fun to watch top players like Federer, Nadal, Djokovic, Murray and the William sisters playing. We enjoyed it so much that we felt like going to other major tennis events. For Mohinder, perhaps playing and watching tennis was one of her favorite retirement activities.

Summer Family Reunions

Every summer since the year 2000, Nina comes from Thailand to Asheville, North Carolina with her children to spend about a month with the whole family. It has been a very special time for us. Everybody looks forward to the summer family fun time. All our grandchildren have natural, close relationships. Esha being the oldest is a wonderful elder sister and leader. Benjamin and Karuna, almost the same age, are great playmates; Camille and Anya get along wonderfully well; and Arjun and Jay are exemplary friends. Jay once postponed his birthday by several months to celebrate when Arjun came from Thailand. They share toys, play games, and seldom have fights or arguments. They care for each other so much that it is always a pleasure to watch them being together as the best of friends. Mohinder enjoyed being with the grandchildren so much that her face would be beaming with happiness which was mutual.

Mohinder with Esha and Jay

During these reunions we had so many activities like going to close by parks, mountain trails, Blue Ridge Parkway, waterfalls and a lot more. Starting close to home, we walked on the trail and had fun in and around the creek. There is a flat rock with water flowing around it with shady trees overhead and rhododendron bushes all around it. It is quite a cool place even on hot days. Children loved this spot for picnics and playing. Once Anya had her birthday party on this rock.

Only a few miles from home, there is another favorite place, a picnic park right on the French Broad River. We had picnics and the children loved to play in the water (very shallow). Next to this park is the North Carolina Arboretum with 65 acres of cultivated flower gardens and hiking trails. The quilt garden represents the quilt craft of the Southern Appalachian region. It is a peaceful place to stroll through, to enjoy and to connect with nature. Besides the botanical gardens it has world class Bonsai Gardens. We used to go and enjoy its beauty, quite often.

Further than the Arboretum, the Blue Ridge Parkway on the southwest side goes to Mount Pisgah which has a beautiful big park with grills and tables for cook outs and play grounds. We used to have picnics and played many games there. Close by there are trails: one going up to the Mount Pisgah summit and the other toward the Pisgah inn through historical hunting grounds. The children loved to go on this trail and learn the history of this area. Pisgah Inn has a very good restaurant for dining. Mount Pisgah was a fun place to spend the whole day.

In the other direction (northeast) the Blue Ridge Parkway goes to Craggy Gardens just before Mount Mitchell Park. We visited Craggy Gardens which are on the top of the mountain. An unpaved trail goes from the parkway to the gardens. However, it was worth walking on the kind of rough and steep trail to enjoy the gardens with beautiful Rhododendrons and other mountain flower beds. It was relatively easy for the children to climb. The view of the mountains from the top is breathtaking.

After these Gardens comes Mount Mitchell State Park on highway 128 from the Parkway. The highway goes all the way to the Mount Mitchell Summit which is 6,684 ft. high. From the parking area there is a paved trail to the observation deck with a romantic 360 degree view of the Blue Ridge Mountains. This was another favorite place for us to enjoy and eat at the restaurant. The restaurant is an excellent government run eating place with a very good Menu including fresh trout (Mohinder's favorite). Further to

Mount Mitchell is Little Switzerland, a small town with a resort and a cafe with southern food, another good place to eat. Close to the town, there are Crab Tree Falls. From the parking area there is a hiking trail to the falls. The falls have a pool at the bottom for children to play in the water. It was very enjoyable for us, especially for the children. It was always fun to drive on the Blue Ridge Parkway and enjoy all these attractions and scenic view of the mountains.

Besides all these fun places, one summer our son-in-law Dr. Mark Groh, arranged an out-door adventure for almost the whole week. It was at River's Way Outdoor Adventure Center, Bluff City, Tennessee. It is a secluded outdoor fun place right on the South Holston River and in the middle of nature. It had rafting, fishing and rope climbing sport for a unique climbing experience. Mark and Sukhdev (Jolly), our son-in-laws, did most of the cooking with some help from us. Mark is an excellent cook with lots of experience in this kind of outdoor situation. The facility is a beautiful place right on the river for rafting when the water is released from the dam which increased the water flow and created rapids. One day we took large rafts for two teams of our family and had a competition in rowing with slogans which was so much fun that all of us had a great time. Mohinder and I were on opposite teams to make the game more competitive. The facility had high rope climbing sport. It was fun to climb and move around on the ropes.

One day, we did the 17 mile bike ride on the Virginia Creeper Trail. We were shuttled from Damascus, to Abingdon, Virginia to start the ride from a high point with the ride ending in Damascus. The bike trail had a gentle slope for an easy ride even for me. Mohinder was one of the leaders riding like a pro. It was a unique experience; however, Bina and Ben had falls. Bina got bruised quite badly. Three good Drs. (Mark, Sumandeep and Nina) came in hand to take care of her and got her going again. With the grace of God our family is quite self-sufficient for most situations. We came back with lots of memories to talk about.

Water Falls

There are beautiful water falls all around the Asheville area. We visited Looking Glass, Sliding Rock, Hookers and DuPont triple falls. All these falls have their own uniqueness for visitors to enjoy.

Looking Glass Falls is on US 276 N, about 6 mile from Brevard, in the Pisgah National Forest. The fall is 60 ft. tall which is accessible by concrete steps with railings. Steps go all the way to the bottom close to the fall. The pool at the bottom of the fall is an excellent place for wading and having fun in the cool water. Mohinder and I mostly sat on the large rocks around the stream while the children did some swimming and wading in the water. The name "Looking Glass" comes from Looking Glass Rock, at the top of the fall, where water freezes around it during winter which shines in the sunlight like a mirror.

Nearby to Looking Glass Falls on the same road is the Sliding Rock Fall, a natural mountain water fall flowing over a 60 ft. flat sloping rock which ends at the 8 ft. deep pool at the bottom. It was a fun place for the children and some of the adults in family. People line up at the top of the fall and one-by-one ride the cold water down into the pool, and swim out for the next person to follow.

DuPont State Recreation Forest is more than 10,000 acres of forest with trails and gorgeous water falls of the Little River namely Hooker Falls, Triple Falls, High Falls and Bridal Veil Falls, in succession from bottom to the top, respectively. The forest is only a 40 mile drive from our home. It is an excellent area for picnicking while enjoying the falls to have fun for the entire day.

There is the Hooker Fall parking area from the DuPont Rd with a trail going to Hooker Falls, only half a mile from the parking lot. There are picnic tables next to the falls. Hooker Falls is only 12 ft. tall; however, it is wide and cascades into a beautiful pool, a popular swimming spot to cool off on hot summer days and then have a picnic on the nearby picnic tables. From here we took the trail to Triple Falls only a mile uphill hike.

Triple Falls, according to their name, is a 120 ft. tall water fall formed of three cascades accessible by steps down to the flat rock plateau between the falls to enjoy the beauty of the fall while walking around. There is a picnic area with tables to eat at this beautiful site. Our family and guests always enjoyed these falls and cherished the memories.

Another interesting and historical place, close to Asheville (52 miles), is Cherokee, NC. It is a town on the Indian Reservation of the Eastern Band of the Cherokee Nation, in Western North Carolina close to the Tennessee border. There is a village showing 18th century Cherokee life style presented in a live performance, "Unto these Hills". It is very informative and educational to learn 18th century American Indian History. Furthermore, there is a Cherokee Museum with artifacts and demonstration of Cherokee life. The Cherokee nation has its own complete language. It was developed by one of the Cherokee, Sequoyah, who created the Cherokee Syllabary for reading and writing the language. There are stores for souvenirs, a restaurant, casino, hotel and a lot more to have an educational fun day. Cherokee people are very proud of their heritage. Our family, especially the grandchildren, enjoyed it very much and learned a lot about Cherokee history.

These are some of the highlights of eleven consecutive family reunions from the year 2000 to 2011. After 2011, our grandchildren were either in college or starting their college education and could not coordinate their summer breaks. These reunions kept the family connected by being together and enjoying one another. Besides our children and grandchildren, Mohinder and I loved it as we could enjoy our grandchildren growing up which made us happy and proud of them. We are so thankful to God for his blessings to have such a loving and caring family.

To keep up with our ancestry, our children and grandchildren love to visit Hoshiarpur and Jande Sarai whenever they are in Panjab. The homes in Hoshiarpur and Jande Sarai have become an attraction for all our children living in foreign countries (America, Thailand, and England). Jande Sarai and the house have become a source of faith and inspiration. We often visit and participate in village projects to stay connected. In 2006, Sumandeep, Bina, Nina, Ben, Camille, Jay and myself visited Jande Sarai and stayed in our home. It was a joyous family reunion as all four brothers, elder sister, cousins and aunts were there to grace the occasion.

Mohinder and I went to Jande Sarai again in Nov. 2012 stayed, slept in our home and enjoyed the hospitality of our relatives. It was Mohinder's third visit to the village. Esha went there in 2014. Her visit was a short one so she wanted to go again and spend more time there, which she did in 2017 along with Bina, Nina and myself.

Chapter 12

MOHINDER THE TRAVELER

By now, Mohinder and I were experienced enough to enjoy travelling to new places. Mohinder was a fun person to travel with as she enjoyed making new friends, and sharing the joys of experiencing new places and people. Her smiling and pleasant manners were a great asset in making friends with strangers.

Our Trip to Alaska was something we talked about ever since we lived in British Columbia. We were planning to celebrate our 46th wedding anniversary by going on a cruise to Alaska. Our daughters heard about it and surprised us about a month before the anniversary. We got a phone call from our travel agent about the Princess Cruise lines tickets to Alaska so that we would not make any other plans on those dates. We appreciated our daughters for the gift and started getting ready to travel.

We flew from Asheville to Anchorage, Alaska. The view of Alaska from the plane was so beautiful with snow covered mountains, wild life, the blue ocean, and snow and ice at many places. From Anchorage, the cruise line bussed us to the ship at Wittier, Alaska. Wittier is about 56 miles southeast of Anchorage. On the way, the bus stopped for snacks and for seeing some Alaskan wildlife such as moose, deer and bear. We were checked in to board the ship. Princess Cruise line ships are very nice. We checked in to our very nice balcony cabin facing the coast line. Our cabin was very well selected in that we had a great view of the mountains, wildlife and glaciers. Mohinder bought high-power binoculars to enjoy a clearer view of wildlife and the glaciers. The ship had all kinds of entertainment such as movies, shows, music and a casino. There were all kinds of good restaurants and a main cafeteria which was open all the time. The food was delicious with an international touch. Restaurants around the pool were nice for drinks and snacks. It was a very comfortable ship. On the first night we cruised to reach the Hubbard Glacier which is nicknamed "Galloping Glacier" as it is rapidly advancing toward the Gulf of Alaska. The glacier is the largest tide water glacier in North America, about 76 miles long plunging 1200 ft. into the depth of the bay. It is beautiful with phenomenal and enchanting blue hues and glorious snow covered mountains in the background. We appreciated this amazing beauty of God's creation and felt that there is so much more to see and appreciate. The ship gave us the best time (6:30 AM) to watch the splashing of the icebergs as they fell into the bay. Mohinder had her binoculars ready and asked me to make sure to wake her up at the right time. We both enjoyed the close-up view which was just amazing. It was an experience, once in lifetime. From our balcony, we watched harbor seals and otters swimming, brown bears, moose and black tailed deer roaming ashore.

Skagway was our next stop to get off the ship and enjoy the town for shopping, eating and to have a lesson in the history of "Gold Rush days". Downtown Skagway was walking distance from our ship. It is a small but important historical town with gold rush era buildings, preserved as part of the Klondike Gold Rush National Historical Park. We visited some museums and souvenir shops and did some shopping, enjoyed lunch with a historical touch while learning about the gold rush.

After Skagway our ship docked at Juneau, the capital of Alaska. We enjoyed walking through this beautiful city, visited the information center, and planned our day. We took a bus tour to Mendenhall Glacier Park. The glacier was a breathtaking sight. We could get quite close to the glacier on the side of the lake. For lunch we enjoyed the special,

Alaskan salmon. We liked walking the self-guided trails. In the afternoon we had dinner with live music. It was a fun day.

Our ship's next stop was Ketchikan, known as the Salmon Capital of the world. It is the southeastern most city of Alaska. The city is named after the Ketchikan Creek which flows through the town with restaurants around it. We enjoyed a seafood lunch sitting outside the restaurant by the creek side. The city has the largest collection of totem poles in the parks. The Totem Heritage Center displays the 19th century totem poles. There are some good jewelry stores for guests from the ship to enjoy. Jewelers were attracting ladies by standing outside the shops and advertising jewelry - one of the items was a Philip Stein watch. The watch has the Natural Frequency technology which helps to regulate the mental body functions such as stress, sleep and mood in general while having a fancy dual time wrist watch. One of the jewelers was from India. He convinced Mohinder (speaking in Hindi) to buy the Philip Stein watch and some other jewelry items. It was another fun city to visit and do shopping.

The Cruise ended in Vancouver British Columbia and we were greeted by a Panjabi lady while going through Canadian Customs. It was a very pleasant ending to the trip. From Vancouver, we flew back to Asheville. The whole trip was a memorable experience which we enjoyed very much.

For our next interesting trip, we planned to celebrate our 50th wedding anniversary in Switzerland and visit some important places in Europe, especially those with Renaissance Art works.

Trip to Europe

After discussing various options for a Europe trip with our travel agent, we decided to take the Essential

Europe tour by Globus Family Bus Company for Italy, Switzerland, France and England. It took us to six important cities: Rome, Florence, Venice, Lucerne, Paris and London. We extended our 10 days trip to 14 to spend two extra days in Rome before the start of the tour to enjoy more of the historical city and two days in London at the end of the tour to visit our relatives, Mohinder's cousin Satinder, my niece Jagprit and nephew Gurkartar.

We flew from Asheville to Rome, Italy. We were in Rome in the afternoon and a Globus Tour representative took us from the airport to the hotel, Michelangelo, just opposite the Vatican City. After checking in, getting freshened up, we got ready for dinner. The hotel clerk gave us the needed information for close by good restaurants and tours of interest for the morning. Some very good restaurants were around the corner and across the street from Vatican City. After enjoying an Italian dinner, we walked around to explore the area and found a Panjabi restaurant whose manager was originally from a city close to my village. He gave us some very good information about how to get around in Rome both by walking and by the city bus service to visit places of interest as well as shop. With all the necessary information, we were well-informed and excited for the next day in Rome. We learned the best resource for information for directions was the policemen. They were easy to communicate with in English and were courteous and informative. We used the city bus service to go around to various places. We visited the castle of Sant Angelo, Roman Forum of the old city including the Caesar palace, the Trevi Fountain and Spanish Steps.

The castle of Saint Angelo, a cylindrical fort, is the mausoleum of roman emperor Hadrian on the right bank of river Tiber. Emperor Hadrian and his family members' and succeeding emperors' ashes are kept in this building. The castle has a nice coffee shop to serve visitors. We enjoyed coffee and snacks with seats by the window with the view of the skyline of Rome. After the tour of the castle, we walked the Aelius Bridge which is decorated with beautiful statues. Then we walked under the bridge and surroundings. While walking around, we met a Roman Soldier impersonator in the park.

With a Roman Solider

After the castle, we visited the Trevi Fountain, one of the most famous fountains in the world. The fountain is a popular place to throw coins for good luck. Approximately 3,000 euros are thrown in daily. The money is used by the city for a supermarket for the needy. The fountain is one of 2,000 fountains in Rome. After seeing the fountain, we walked to the Spanish Steps, another interesting tourist attraction. In the street, we met a vendor selling freshly roasted chestnuts, one of our favorite snacks. Those chestnuts were a delicious afternoon snack. Then we reached the Spanish Steps, 135 steps with a beautiful fountain at the bottom and a church at the top.

At Trevi Fountain

At St. Angelo Castle

At Tiber River

Well-come Globus Dinner

In the evening, our tour started with a three-course dinner with live music in a classy Italian restaurant across the river. Besides the dinner, it was a chance to meet and greet all the co-travelers on the tour. All the tourists were friendly, an international group of people, Americans, Australian and New Zealanders. Our tour in Rome was to visit Vatican Museums, St. Peter's Square and Basilica, Colosseum, and the Roman Forum.

Vatican City was a much desired part of the trip, especially for Mohinder to see Michelangelo's world famous paintings of the Sistine Chapel ceiling. We had a guided tour of Vatican City with a very knowledgeable guide who explained every part of the tour very well.

In Art Gallery

Sistine Chapel

St. Peters Square, Pope blessing the visitors

Vatican Museums display art work collections of popes throughout the centuries, formed of sculptures and masterpieces of Renaissance art. Pope Julius the II founded the museums. It has 54 art galleries. Walking through the galleries was very informative for Mohinder. She was stopping and asking all kinds of art questions and enjoying every moment of the tour. Finally we reached the Sistine Chapel, the high light of our tour. It was so exciting to see the ceiling of which we had seen so many pictures before. Our guide seated us and explained the art work. She told us that Michelangelo did not originally paint underwear on male paintings. Those were done later by another artist, Daniele da Volterra. The two walls and the ceiling are painted beautifully to depict the history of Christianity. Botticelli painted the two long walls and Michelangelo the ceiling which illustrates stories from the book of Genesis from the creation of the world to the story of Noah. It was an eye opener for us. This museum is one of the most visited art museums in the world. About 5 million people visit it every year.

While in St. Peter's Square, we had quite a close view of Pope Benedict XVI standing in his pope mobile blessing the devotees. The tour of the Vatican was very interesting and informative. We often had talked about visiting and seeing the famous renaissance art work, especially the Sistine Chapel ceiling in Rome.

After Vatican we visited the Colosseum and Roman Forum. The Colosseum is an ancient roman amphitheater. It is a three tiered building of Roman Empire to entertain emperors, their families and dignitaries. The building has 80 arched entrances with the seating for 55,000 people who were seated according to their ranks. The amphitheater staged deadly combats of wild animals and gladiators (professional fighters usually slaves, criminals or prisoners of war). These cruel gams were stopped as Christianity progressed in Italy.

Roman Forum is a rectangular plaza located at the center of Rome between Palatine and Capitoline hills. It is surrounded by the well preserved important ruins of ancient government buildings and palaces of the emperors. We visited the ruins of the Julius Caesar palace. There is lots of history of the mighty Roman Empire in the forum. It is another tourist attractions in Rome attracting about 4.5 million visitors annually.

Roman Forum

After enjoying the tour of Rome and a delicious dinner we had a good night's sleep. Next morning we had an early breakfast and had an easy ride north to Florence, the cradle of the Renaissance. Florence is a large city, capital of Italy's Tuscany region. It was the center of the medieval European trade thus one of the richest cites in Europe. It is considered the birth place of the Renaissance. It attracts a large number of tourists every year, perhaps to see Michelangelo's famous sculpture of David, another attraction Mohinder was excited to see.

We enjoyed a walking tour with a local guide and visited the Academy of Fine Arts which houses Michelangelo's celebrated David. David is a 17ft tall marble statue weighing 12, 478 pounds, of a standing male nude, representing the biblical hero David. It is a masterpiece of renaissance sculpture created in years 1501-1504. At first the statue was placed in a public square outside the town hall of Florence. Later on, due to political reasons, it was moved to a more secure place, the Academy of Fine Arts and a replica was placed in the square. There are several replicas of David all over the city. One of the friends in our group commented after seeing some of these statues, "This nude has taken over the whole town. If I will dare to be like him in a public place, police will arrest and put me in jail." Hearing the comment, we had the best laugh of the day.

David in the city square

After seeing a lot of art works in the Academy, we visited a magnificent Cathedral, Giotto's Bell Tower, the heavy bronze Gate of Paradise, and the Signoria Square dotted with gorgeous sculptures everywhere. From here we walked over the famous old bridge (Ponte Vecchio), the oldest bridge over the river Arno in Florence. It is covered and has various types of shops such as jewelry and souvenirs. On the east side of the bridge there are very good Italian restaurants. We enjoyed delicious seafood and walked around to do some shopping. Suddenly, we were greeted by a Panjabi gentleman. He showed us the menu and invited us to his restaurant. We said, "Some other time" as we already had our lunch. There is a beautiful fountain on the east end of the bridge with a bust statue of Benvenuto Cellini, in its center.

River Arno

Fountain with the statue

From there we walked to the Basilica of the Holy Cross, the temple of the Italian Glories which is the burial place of some famous Italians such as Michelangelo and Galileo. The guide explained and showed us the graves which are underground. Visitors need to be properly dressed to show respect. We had a young girl in our group who was refused entry as she had shorts on. She was so sad; Mohinder gave her over shirt to the young lady to wrap around over her shorts. It worked and she was allowed to enter. That girl and her parents appreciated Mohinder for the help and became close friends for the rest of our tour.

At Gate to Heaven

Temple of the Italian Glories, Michelangelo's grave

From Florence our bus went through the Apennine hills and the plains of the mighty river Po to Venice. We crossed Grand Canal of Venice in a private boat to St. Mark's Square. Venice is a unique city built on more than 100 small islands in a marshy lagoon in the Adriatic Sea. The Grand Canal snakes through the city connecting important places in the city and homes by numerous narrow channels, which are like streets, accessible by boats. Boats are used like cars are in other places.

On the bridge on a small canal

In St. Mark's square with pigeons

Ready to see the homes in Venice

Ready to explore Venice

In St. Mark's Square we visited the Byzantine Basilica, the Clock Tower, and lavish Doges' Palace and the Bridge of Sighs. We toured a glass blowing shop and watched the artists making beautiful glass objects. We took a boat ride through the city and saw homes with boats to go around. It was a unique experience.

Our tour guide recommended the famous Harry's Bar/ restaurant for eating in St. Mark's square. We enjoyed a meal with good service and quality food at Harry's. We heard it was a favorite restaurant of Ernest Hemingway, the famous writer. Numerous pigeons in St. Mark's Square were very friendly, and would sit on the shoulders and arms of tourists. Mohinder had lots of fun with them. It seemed like they were her pets.

After Venice, we headed to Lucerne, Switzerland through the Lombardian Plains, past Milan and Lake Como to the Swiss Alps.

Enjoying the view of the Alps

Snacking in a café on the Alps

We stopped in Lugano and had coffee with a stunning view of mountains all around. Then while going through the towering Swiss Alps and passing through St. Gotthard, we reached Lucerne, a beautiful Swiss Town on the north end of Lake Lucerne. It is a 14th century town in central Switzerland.

Dinner in Lucerne

We walked through the lake side park and had tea. River Rouse flows through the town. It has the famous covered wooden Kallbrucke Bridge (Chapel Bridge) connecting St. Peter's Chapel with the town. It is a one of a kind diagonal bridge with shops.

Our hotel was within walking distance from the bridge and shopping mall and other retail centers. It was a good place to spend money. Mohinder bought a lovely Tissot Swiss wrist watch for me as a wedding anniversary present. We strolled the city streets and visited the famous Lion Monument, a dying Lion Statue commemorating the death of 26 soldiers and more than 700 troops of the Swiss guards who died while protecting King Louis XVI.

Dying Lion Monument

We took a panoramic Gondola ride to Mount Pilatus, 7,000 ft. up. At the top there is a breathtaking view of the snow covered Alps, and a very nice café. We had coffee and snacks and walked around to enjoy the scenery. It was the 7th of June, our 50th wedding anniversary.

Base of Mount Pilatus

On Mount Pilatus

Enjoying coffee on top of Mt. Pilatus

In the evening, we treated ourselves to a three course Swiss dinner with the culture of Swiss Folklore, Alphorns, yodeling and traditional instrumental music. It was a very enjoyable evening. It turned out to be an even better anniversary than we imagined.

Anniversary dinner with Swiss music show

After a good night's sleep and a memorable anniversary, we headed toward Paris, France. We crossed into France while enjoying a ride through the vineyards of Burgundy and Fontainebleau forest. We reached Paris to tour this famous city of the Eiffel Tower and the capital of France, with so much to offer tourists.

After a French dinner, our tour guide took us to see the Eiffel Tower with its evening lights. It was much different than during the day.

Eiffel Tower at night

With Eiffel Tower at night

At the base of Eiffel Tower

The next day we visited the Eiffel Tower again. A wrought iron lattice tower named after the engineer Gustave Eiffel. He designed and built it as the entrance to the World's Fair of 1889. The tower is 984 ft. high with a square base of 410ft.on each side. It is one of the tallest structures in Paris and one of the most visited monuments in the world. We spent most of the morning doing some shopping on the second floor of this huge tower and enjoyed a French lunch in a restaurant. After that, we visited the Paris markets and enjoyed a snack close to the Opera House, a beautiful opera theater with lots of history. We visited the Arc de Triumph, Notre Dame Cathedral and a lot more in a short time.

In front of Charles Garnier Statue

In the Opera House

Enjoying a break across the street of the Opera House

With Paris in the background

At night for dinner we went to La Nouvelle Eve Cabaret in Paris, an international dinner show with dancing girls and live music in Pigalle. It featured entertainment and dining from 6:30PM to midnight. It was expensive; however, it was worth the money.

The next morning, we were grateful to our bus driver for his excellent job of driving from Rome to Paris. I asked Mohinder about a tip for the driver and suggested 50 dollars. She said, "Give him 100 dollars. He did such a good job." So I did and the driver gave us a nice thank you and a smile.

We boarded the Eurostar Train, for a fast ride from Paris to London, which arrived in London in the afternoon. We checked in at the Hilton London Metropole, a hotel in the Asian neighborhood and close to most of the London attractions. After getting ready we had a gourmet dinner at Christopher's restaurant followed by the musical, "Billy Elliot", at the Victoria Palace Theater. Walking around at night in London was quite interesting to see the city with lights and reflections of buildings in the Thames River.

The next day we did the sightseeing with a local guide to visit some famous land marks: Knightsbridge, the House of Parliament, Big Ben Clock Tower, Westminster Abbey, and Buckingham Palace with the changing of the guards and St. Paul's Cathedral. It was a lot to see in one day. Although we had stops for lunch and coffee breaks for needed rest, it was still tiring. We enjoyed the London tour so much and learned a lot about the city. London, the capital of the United Kingdom/Britain, is one of most important cities of the world.

Outside the St. Paul's Cathedral

In front of Buckingham Palace

London is where the once mighty British Empire was ruled from. The empire included India and North America as well. By 1922 the British Empire ruled about 458 million people all over the world. It was almost one fourth of the earth's surface. At the peak of its rule, there was a phrase "The sun never sets in the British Empire" which was used to describe the extent of their realm. As compared to what was the British Empire, the United Kingdom of Great Britain has an area of only 93, 600 sq. miles. We both were very interested to see London together (we visited London separately before) as we both had the experience of living in India under British rule until 1947 when India gained its freedom. Mohinder and I were 8 and 15 years old respectively and remembered a lot about the Indian Freedom Movement.

That night we had a farewell dinner at our hotel. We exchanged our contact information and felt like saying farewell to our tour friends. Some people even cried while hugging each other. It was an interesting, historical, and very informative tour with a lot to learn and a lot to do in 2 short weeks. Our tour guide did a great job throughout the tour for us to have fun and stay safe in all the new places.

The next morning, the tour members had breakfast at the hotel and the tour ended. We were picked up by my niece, Jagpreet and her husband, Harmeet (Lucky) from the hotel. We spent the day with them and enjoyed their hospitality and did some shopping and visited the nearby Gurdwara Nanak Sar Sahib for prayer and gratitude for God's blessings.

The next day we were picked up by my nephew, Gurkartar and his wife. We visited Mohinder's cousin, Satinder and enjoyed our visit and a delicious lunch. We spent the evening with Gurkartar's family. We had a delightful dinner and enjoyed the company of their daughter, my grandniece. We met her for the first time. She was majoring in Chemistry for her graduate studies. She is a brilliant person and another shining star in our family.

Two weeks of touring Europe was one of our best historical adventures viewing world famous art work, and a comprehensive experience in seeing important places, meeting interesting people and enjoying exotic foods to celebrate our 50th wedding anniversary and Mohinder's 70th birthday. It was an unforgettable tour to six historical cities in four different countries. Furthermore to our surprise, it was a wedding anniversary gift from our very thoughtful daughters. We are blessed with such a wonderful and generous family.

Panama Canal Cruise

After the Europe trip, we planned our next trip to the Panama Canal, one of the great engineering achievements of the twentieth century. The canal created a great short cut for mariners by connecting the Atlantic and Pacific Oceans in Central America. Before this, they travelled around the southern tip of South America (Chile and Argentina). Due to our previous good experience, we took the Princess Panama Canal Cruise in November, 2010. This time Bina, our daughter, accompanied us.

We drove to Ft. Lauderdale and visited our friend, Dr. Kirpal Singh on the way in Orange Port, Florida and spent the night there. The next morning, we drove to Ft. Lauderdale and arrived there in the afternoon, checked into our hotel and had a good night's sleep. Next afternoon, we were picked up by the Princess Cruise Lines van to board the ship. We checked into our Balcony Cabin which was very nice and comfortable. We had a tour of the ship to know all there was to enjoy for the next 10 days. As expected the ship had all the fun things: restaurants, swimming pools, lounges, shows, movies and casinos, etc. Besides visiting various places off the ship, we had a lot of fun on the ship while cruising. After cruising for two days, we reached Oranjestad (orange town) the capital of Aruba, a state of the kingdom of Netherland.

Aruba is a small island (20 miles long and 6 miles wide at its widest point) in the Southern Caribbean Sea. Being outside the hurricane belt and with temperatures around 82 degrees Fahrenheit all year round, it is a popular destination for tourists.

Oranjestad is a unique town with buildings and houses painted in various bright colors such as lime, red, yellow, orange and green. We visited a park with beautiful flowers and the statue of Queen Wilhelmina of Netherland.

Statue of queen of Netherland

City Street with colorful building

There were iguanas, the largest we ever saw (size of baby alligators), almost everywhere along the coast line. We walked around the town and visited a restaurant for tea and shops for souvenirs. We had only a few hours stop in this town. However, we enjoyed this interesting Dutch community with beautiful colorful buildings, well maintained parks and sandy beaches.

Our next stop was Cartagena, Columbia. We got off the ship and had only six hours to visit this beautiful historical Colombian city with a lot to see. We were told by the ship information office to rent a taxi with driver who would be tour guide as well. As we got off the ship there was a large taxi stand with drivers advertising to be hired. Some of them were quite pushy and trying to impress us with their English language. There was a nice and relatively quiet young man with less fluent English. While we were talking to him, some other drivers told us that he was not a good guide as his English was very poor.

We liked the driver and he told us that he would charge us forty American dollars for the day. We agreed and told him that we would pay him fifty dollars for the taxi ride and tour of the city. He was one happy man. His taxi was quite comfortable. We started the tour of city which is formed of two parts, an old walled city, and the modern city.

Cartagena is a port city on the northern coast of Colombia, with a population of about one million. It is one of the largest cities in Colombia. The old part is a colonial walled city and fortress with plazas, cobblestone streets and colonial historical buildings. It was designated a UNESCO heritage site. Our guide took us to most of the tourist attractions. We visited the old business area, museum, San Diego Park with statues, Felipe de Barajas and Cartagena's wide and thick fort wall with cannons mounted all around, facing the ocean. It was a very educational tour of the old city.

Cartagena old city

After the old city, our guide took us through the new city with modern residential and business areas. It has beautiful houses, shopping plazas and three to five star hotels (with quite reasonable prices) and good restaurants to make tourists quite comfortable. We asked our friendly guide to take us to one of the best restaurants in town with fish as its specialty. He took us to a very nice and clean restaurant. There were quite a few tourists in the restaurant enjoying their meal. We felt good about this choice, checked the menu and ordered the local fish. It was a good meal, with good service.

We visited many places and saw a lot of this city of the old Spanish Empire. Our driver brought us back to the ship. We thanked him for a job well done. I said, "Mohinder, let us pay him 60 dollars." She said, "Pay him 100 dollars." Bina also nodded in the affirmative. I gave him a 100 dollar bill and thanked him for being such a good and pleasant guide and driver. He was one happy person, with a million dollar thankful smile. We were back on the ship, having had a wonderful experience.

The next day, early morning, we were cruising through Panama Canal, the highlight of the trip. The canal is a man made 50 mile waterway in Panama, South America, connecting the Atlantic Ocean (Caribbean Sea) on the east to the Pacific Ocean (Gulf of Panama) on the west, across the Isthmus of Panama. France started the work on the canal in 1887 and stopped due to the high mortality of workers and engineering problems. The United States of America took over the project in 1904 and completed it in 1914. Due to some serious excavation problems an artificial lake, Gatun Lake, was created on the east side by building a dam on the river. The lake is about 87 ft. above sea level. To overcome this water level between the two oceans, there are three sets of lock gates with troughs on each side of the Gatun Lake to lower and raise the cruising ships by three steps both ways. On the east side of Gutan Lake are three Gutan lock gates and on the west side of the lake are Pedro Miguel lock gate, and Mira Flores Lake lock gates.

Panama Canal

Approximately 17,500 ships pass through the canal annually by paying about 1.8 billion dollars in toll. It takes 8-10 hrs. to sail through the canal.

    The United States controlled the canal and surrounding territory from 1904 to 1999. Now it is under the control of Panama. The canal created a tremendous and very safe short cut between the Atlantic and Pacific oceans for mariners. For example, for a ship to go from San Francisco to New York used to take 13,000 miles to go around the southern tip of South America (Brazil and Argentina). Now through the Panama Canal it takes only 5,200 miles with safe cruising and it is quite economical as well.

    The Panama Canal is one of the best engineering achievements of the modern era. To express this accomplishment appropriately, the American Society of

Civil Engineers has called the Panama Canal the 7th wonder of the modern world.

    While cruising through the canal, we watched the operation of the lock gates and filling and emptying of their respective troughs to raise and lower the ship, step by step. It was an amazing experience to go from one ocean to another in such a short time. The Panama Canal is really a manmade engineering marvel of modern times.

    Close to the end of the Panama Canal cruising, our ship docked at Colon, Panama. Colon is a Panama's seaport city near the Atlantic entrance to the Panama Canal. The city was founded by Americans in 1850 as the Atlantic terminal of the Panama railroad. The city is named in honor of Christopher Columbus.

    It was a short three hour stop and Mohinder had some stomach problems. Therefore only Bina and I went out to the town and walked around the communities and houses with iron gates. People seemed to be friendly and happy. There were a few street events with Calypso music which was quite rhythmic and harmonic, we stopped to enjoy the music. We did some shopping and hurried back to see how Mohinder was feeling. Mohinder was feeling much better after resting. After dinner, we went to a magic show. After enjoying the very amusing magic tricks, we decided to go to a movie. It was a very entertaining evening. The next day our ship docked at Limon, Costa Rica, with an eleven hr. stop.

Limon (means lemon in Spanish), an eastern sea port of Costa Rico was discovered by Christopher Columbus in 1502. It is the sixth largest city in Costa Rica with a population of 55,000 people of Afro-Caribbean origin, speaking Spanish and Limonese Creole.

We took a 6 hr. Greenway Bus tour to see the rain forest and a banana plantation. Our tour guide, a very nice lady (speaking good English) was explaining interesting things, describing working village folks and their homes with beautiful flowery yards on the way to the rain forest canal tour. She spotted various wildlife animals such as two and three toed sloths on trees, howler monkeys, herons, egrets and hawks.

After reaching our destination, which was a boat docking building with eating and other essential facilities, we were treated to a local tropical fruit snack with live Calypso music.

Snacking with live music

We took the boat to go through the rain forest canal, with attractive homes having their fishing boats in the canal and cars in their yards. There were quite high mountains on both sides of the canal. We saw numerous poisonous frogs and other wild life in those mountains.

Due to very heavy rain during the boat ride, it was hard to enjoy the wild-life as they were not very active. The boat took us very close to the ocean. After the boat tour, we had fish and local foods with an excellent live Calypso band. It was a very satisfying lunch, an interesting tour and lively entertainment.

Next we rode the bus to the banana plantation tour. On our way a very courteous sweet old lady, in a road side fruit stand, gave each of us a ripe and delicious small banana. We bought some of the bananas and thanked her. At the banana plantation, we were given a tour of the plantation with banana bunches at different stages of ripening from quite green to picking stage. After the plantation, we visited the packing warehouse/factory with the explanation of the whole process from picking, storing, packing and shipping the fruit. It was a very informative tour and we learned where some of the bananas in stores come from.

The bus driver and the tour guide did a good job throughout the day. We were back in time for some shopping. We visited a mall close to the ship and bought some Costa Rican coffee and souvenirs. As it was raining, it was hard to enjoy the shopping. We returned to the ship quite wet and remembering the damp weather of the rain forest. Our next stop was Grand Cayman. We were excited to visit another Caribbean city close to Jamaica. We booked some interesting tours to enjoy this city. We had planned almost a full day of sightseeing, shopping and tasting the local foods.

We were disappointed after reaching the Grand Cayman port when told that the docking had been refused by the port authorities due to bad weather and very rough seas. We could see the sky lines of the city from the ship. After waiting several hours our ship started sailing back to Fort Lauderdale. There was a young couple on the ship who had plans to be wedded in Grand Cayman. They were heart broken when the ship started sailing back. This was the only sad part of our cruise. All in all, it was a great trip with lots of interesting, historical and informative tours to enjoy.

A Trip through Southeast Asia

In 2011, after a summer reunion of the whole Sarai family in Asheville, we planned another trip through Southeast Asia for seven weeks to Thailand and India. This time we planned almost a month in India to visit all the relatives, visiting Gurdwaras to pay our respects and a grand celebration of birthdays of all four Sarai brothers at our newly rebuilt ancestral home in our native village, Jande Sarai. There was a lot of excitement to have this fun trip. We got ready for the journey and for precautionary measure we made doctor's appointments for general checkups. On Dec. 28, 2011, Mohinder was diagnosed with breast cancer.

The whole family was shocked, and then concentrated on the best treatment for Mohinder. Sumandeep and her husband, Dr. Mark Groh, arranged the surgery and all the required tests done within a week. Mohinder needed radiation of the affected area, and taking the inhibiting medicine to stop the disease from reoccurring. After all this, Mohinder was given 15 years of a good and healthy life. This was very encouraging good news.

Considering the situation, our trip was rescheduled for Oct- Dec. 2012. For a celebration of Mohinder's health, a short trip to Cambodia to see the famous Angkor region, and a visit to Jaipur (pink City), Rajasthan India were added to the trip. Mohan auntie planned to visit India with us to celebrate Diwali and participate in the Bhai Dooj Tikka Ceremony at Amritsar.

We reached Thailand on Oct 10, 2012 and enjoyed all the excitement with Nina's family to see Mohinder in good health and in a great mood. Nina had arranged a 4-day trip to Cambodia. Within three days, we all flew to Siem Reap, Cambodia. It was a short flight from Thailand. After customs clearance at Siem Reap airport, we were taxied to the Hotel (a resort outside the main city). We checked into this beautiful facility with individual units and all the amenities such as a swimming pool, massage parlor, gym and a beautiful pool side restaurant. It was a very comfortable place for vacationing.

Siem Reap is the capital of Siem Reap province of Cambodia, and home of the magnificent historical Angkor ruins: Angkor Wat and Angkor Thom, of the Khmer civilization. These ruins are recognized by UNESCO as one of the world's heritage sites. Thus it is a popular destination for tourists. About one million people visit this place annually, which is a good source of income for the area.

Next morning after a delicious breakfast including seasonal fresh fruit, we headed out to tour Angkor Wat. Angkor Wat is a complex with one of the largest Hindu temples in the world. The complex occupies about 400 acres of a square walled area. In the center is the main temple with several other buildings around it. It is the largest religious monument in the world. It was built by King Surya Varman II (1112-1152) of the Khmer Empire. Apparently he had extensive knowledge of Hindu Mythology as the temple represents the scenes from the beginning of the world to the present in the form of sculptures and intricate carvings.

The front entrance has an 11ft. high Statue of the God Vishnu. The walls around the entrance have 3000 sculptures of Apsaras. They are mythical beautiful supernatural heavenly female dancers. They dance to the music of court musicians of the God Indra. The inner wall of the outer gallery has beautiful carvings representing detailed scenes of Hindu scriptures, the Ramayana and the Mahabharata. From the Ramayana, it is the account of the battle of Lanka in which Sri Ram Chandar JI (Lord Rama), with the help of Lord Hanuman with an army of monkeys, defeated Ravan (Ravana) the king of Lanka. From the Mahabharata, it is the description of the battle of Kurukshatra in which Pandavas defeated Kauravas.

The Bhagavad Gita, a Hindu Scripture, is the description (700 verses) of a dialogue between Pandava Prince Arjun and his guide and Charioteer Sri Krishan Bhagwan Ji (Lord Krishna) in the battle of Kurukshatra. Arjun is counseled by Lord Krishna to fulfill his duty as a warrior in a righteous war against his unjust relatives, Kauravas. Arjun fought and the Pandavas defeated the Kauravas. Both Lord Rama and Lord Krishna are considered reincarnations of the God Vishnu. The Angkor Wat temple is also known as a temple of the God Vishnu.

The central temple is formed of three stories. Each floor encloses a central square surrounded by various chambers. The stairs to the upper level are very steep and quite hard to climb as this level is considered the kingdom of Gods. The central temple has five towers, one central, which is the tallest and four smaller corner towers. The central tower rises 180 ft. above the ground level. These towers are visible from the distance as an impressive scene of Angkor Wat.

Mohinder was very impressed with the art work representing the detailed stories of Hindu mythology. We learned so much about Hinduism at this one site.

The family outside the main Temple

Enjoying a break on the second Floor of Angkor Wat

The next day, we visited Angkor Thom (meaning great city) which was the last capital of the Khmer Empire. These are the ruins of the ancient city, with detailed displays of sculptures and carvings depicting Gods, Goddesses and numerous stories related to them and other present day animals related to those stories from the ancient Hindu mythology. Some of those were somewhat modified later by Buddhism, the state religion since the 13th century. It is believed that this beautiful city during its glory days had over 80,000 population.

The city is on the west bank of the Siem Reap River covering about 3.5 square miles of area surrounded by a 7.2 mile long and 26 ft. high wall. The wall is enclosed by a 328 ft. wide trench which used to be filled with water and crocodiles to protect the city. There is a gate in the middle of each wall with a bridge over the trench leading to a road. The south gate leads to Angkor Wat and was the most used gate. The gate has sculptures of Demons on one side and Angels on the other holding a serpent, like tug of war, to churn the ocean. They represent a mythological story of churning the ocean, by using a serpent as a rope and a mountain as a rod, to extract the 14 gems.

Within the walls there are several monuments from its early era, as well as those established by king Jayavarman VII (AD 1125-1218) who founded the city. There is so much ancient Hindu history at this amazing site. We, especially Mohinder being an artist, enjoyed our visit of this remarkable historical place.

Entering Angkor Thom

In the center is the state temple, Bayon, with other monuments around it. The state temple represents the intersection of earth and heaven. It has four high towers, one at each corner, with four huge stone faces of the Lord Bodhisattva Avalokitesvara, Buddhist deity (embodiment of Buddha Compassion) with one facing each of the four directions, thus keeping watch at all the directions. There are 51 smaller towers surrounding the temple, each with four faces of its own.

Mohinder enjoying the art work face to face.

After enjoying the Angkor sites, we were ready to visit the city for shopping, fun things like getting our feet cleaned by dipping them into a tank with small fish, and enjoying some authentic Cambodian dishes. People were very friendly and communicating quite well in English. We went to museums and shopping malls for souvenirs and clothing. It was fun and very enjoyable to walk around in this interesting city. We appreciated Nina and Jolly for arranging this interesting trip.

We came back to Bangkok to rest for a few days and to get ready for the trip to India. We planned to spend about four weeks, enough time, to see relatives, from both sides of the family, who were so excited and anxious to see Mohinder after about fourteen years.

Trip to India

We reached Delhi, the first week of November and stayed with Mohinder's cousins. Besides spending time with relatives and being treated to their hospitality, we visited historical Sikh Gurdwaras, Sis Ganj Sahib, Rakab Ganj Sahib and Bangla Sahib to offer our thanks, respect and prayers for all the blessings, especially Mohinder's health. It was a great and blissful feeling. Then we spent a few days sight-seeing and shopping. We enjoyed lots of hospitality and a great time with relatives in Delhi. Mohan auntie was a great companion taking us to various relatives as she visits them quite often and had their addresses and contact information. We were just tagging along and enjoying ourselves. For further help Kiran, wife of Mohinder's cousin Tejinder Singh Arora, accompanied us. Our daughter, Dr. Nina Srikureja joined us after about a week in Delhi. In the meantime, we had visited all our relatives there. We made plans for the next leg of our journey, Jaipur visit, our team of five, Kiran quite familiar with Jaipur, Mohan auntie a great friend of Mohinder and a diplomat, Nina a medical Doctor, and myself to keep them company were all well prepared for this trip. We took the train to Jaipur, the pink city, which is another tourist attraction, in India. It is only 156 miles from Delhi. The train ride was quite comfortable. It was very enjoyable to see the country side of Rajasthan State with people working in the fields and little children playing and watching the train going by. After reaching Jaipur railway station, we hired a taxi for our stay in Jaipur. He was our tour guide as well.

Jaipur is the capital of Rajasthan state of India. It is named after its founder raja Jai Singh II, the ruler of Amer (now Jaipur) state. He ruled the state from 1688-1758. He founded the city in 1727. The city was designed by consulting Hindu Scriptures and was divided into nine blocks with two for state buildings and palaces and the other seven for public use. Later in 1876 the city was changed to its pink color (British Empire's map color) to welcome the Prince of Wales, later King Edward VII of the British Empire who ruled from 1901-1910.

Perhaps the pink color was used to show the loyalty of the state to the British Empire. Many of the Avenues are still pink and the city is popularly called Pink City. The city houses three renowned Rajasthan colleges, several palaces, forts and museums and a lot more to keep tourists happily busy and entertained. The economy of Jaipur depends on tourism, gemstone cutting, jewelry and luxury textiles.

After getting settled in the hotel, we were ready to tour the historic city. Next morning, our driver took us to the main attractions of Jaipur. We started with the tour of Amer Fort which was followed by Jal Mahal.

Amer Fort/Amer palace is in the Amer city. It is about 7 miles from Jaipur on the top of the Hill of Eagles. Amer was the capital of the state before Jaipur. The fort was built by Raja Man Singh, nephew of Princess Jodha Bai, who was married to Emperor Akbar. Jodha Bai was born in Amer in 1542 and was married to Akbar in 1562. Thus she became the queen of India. Akbar named her Marriam-uz-Zamani. She gave birth to crown prince Salem who became Emperor Jahangir in 1605 after the death of his father Emperor Akbar. This relationship united these rulers of Rajasthan with the Mughal Empire which strengthened the Mughal rule in India. Raja Man Singh was one of the Nava Ratanas (meaning nine gems). They were nine genius men of Emperor Akbar's court. He was also an army general who carried out Emperor Akbar's orders very diligently. The well-known quote from the Movie, Mughal-a- Azam, "Man Singh Hukam- ki- Tameel Ho". The quote means Man Singh my (Akbar's) orders should be obeyed, explains the kind of relationship they had.

Amer Fort houses various buildings of prominence such as Shila Devi temple, Sheesh Mahal, Diwan-i- Aam, and many more to function as residences and administrative locations of the rulers. These buildings represent both Rajput and Islamic architectural styles.

The first structure of interest in the fort was the Shila Devi temple. It has the Idol of the Goddess Durga/ Kali which has been worshipped by the Rajas. Our fort guide told us that the offerings to the Goddess are a goat and hard liquor early in the morning. At certain times of the day the temple is open to the public and preachers distribute some of those offerings to the devotees. Luckily we reached the temple at one of those visitation times. There was a big crowed of people in front of the temple, some with bottles of whiskey. Mohinder was interested to visit the temple for that she stood in line for quite some time and then gave up. She was quite disappointed.

After walking through buildings and gardens we reached Sheesh Mahal, Mirror Palace, perhaps the most popular and beautiful part of the Amer Fort. The walls and ceiling of the hall are carved with beautiful paintings and flowers made of pure glass and precious stones. Because of these small mirrors, if two candles are lit in the middle of the hall then the reflection from these mirrors converts the palace into a bright place with thousands of stars, an awesome effect similar to the sky filled with twinkling stars on a clear night. This palace is so well known that the famous movie, Mughal-e- Azam, was shot at this site. Some other popular movies regarding Mughal rule have also been filmed here. Mohinder enjoyed the Mughal style of art work as some of her paintings are of this style.

In Sheesh Mahal

We saw the Diwan-a-Aam and many other buildings, and appreciated the living style of Rajas and their queens. There are museums displaying their clothes and other belongings. Diwan-a- Aam was the public court to conduct the business of the rulers. It reminded me of similar buildings in Mughal forts, such as Red Fort Delhi, Agra Fort and Fatehpur Sikri fort.

There was a lot to see and experience of this historical fort which influenced the Mughal Empire in India, and the struggle for the freedom from it. On the way about four miles from the city is the Jal Mahal, meaning Water Palace. It is a five story building in the middle of the Man Sagar Lake. Only the top story is above the water. It is a beautiful sight with mountains in the back ground.

With Mohan Auntie and Nina in front of Jal Mahal.

It also was quite an interesting, historical and informative tour. By now, we were tired and ready to relax and have some dinner in a good restaurant. We treated ourselves to some local cuisine and live music in a good restaurant (recommended by the driver). After dinner, we did some shopping and walked around in the center of the city.

Next morning, we got ready for some more sightseeing. This time it was the famous Jaipur observatory and the city palace. The observatory known as Jantar Mantar, meaning calculating instruments, is a collection of nineteen architectural masonry and brass instruments to observe astronomical positions of various cosmological objects with the naked eye. It was built by Raja Jai Singh in 1734 based on the principles of ancient Hindu Scriptures. It has the world's largest Sun Dial giving very accurate time. Our tour guide explained the use of various instruments with calculation instructions. It was amazing to know the way these scientific astronomical calculations were done in the eighteenth century with limited technical means to work with.

Sundial at Jantar Mantar

Close to the observatory is the City Palace which was our next stop. The palace is a complex housing several important buildings: Chandra Mahal (Palace), Mubark Mahal, Diwan-i- Khas, Diwan-i-Aam, court yards and gardens which served as the residence and administrative centers of the Rajas.

Palace Entrance

Chandra Mahal is a seven story building which houses many unique paintings, mirror work on the walls and floral decorations. Only the ground floor is allowed for visiting. On this floor is the museum displaying various items which belonged to the royal family. The palace is presently used as the residence of the decedents of Jaipur Rajas. Once emperor Aurangzeb (grandson of Emperor Jahangir), great grandson of Jodha Bai, attended the wedding of Raja Jai Singh and shook his hands and conferred the title Sawai, meaning one and a quarter, which had been used by the Rajas of Jaipur as a prefix with their names such as Raja Sawai Jai Singh.

Mubark Mahal was the reception center to welcome important guests, especially Mughal Rulers and English dignitaries. The architecture of this building is a mixture of Rajput, Islamic and European styles. This palace houses a museum with belongings of the Rajas such as clothes worn by Raja Madho Singh, a big person, weighing 550 lbs. with a 48 inches waist. It was interesting to know the size of some these Rajas.

Diwan-i-Khas was a private audience hall of the Rajas. There are two huge shining sterling silver vessels (Each 5.3 ft. high, 1057 gallons in volume and weighing 750 lbs.) on display in this hall. These vessels were made in 1901 for Raja Madho Singh II to carry his drinking water from the River Ganges for his trip to England to attend the Coronation Ceremony of King Edward VII in 1902. Being a pious Hindu, he did not like to drink the English water.

There is a Diwan-i-Aam or the hall of public audience in the courtyard of Mubarak Mahal. Amer Fort and Jaipur Observatory are selected by UNESCO as world Heritage sites. Jaipur is one of the popular tourist destinations in India being visited by about 5,000 visitors daily. In the evening, we visited Chokhi Dhani, meaning a special village. It is an excellent theme park representing authentic Rajasthan country life. It is another important attraction in Jaipur which is considered a must to complete the Jaipur visit.

Chokhi Dhani, is a resort with cottages for vacationing, facilities for business meetings, wedding halls, massage parlors, gymnasium, and shops with souvenirs and clothing. They have specials for one day visit with dinner. We purchased the one day tour. There was lots of entertainment present and a planned Rajasthan dinner. We saw magicians, acrobats, snake charmers, puppet shows, plays, live music, bullock cart and camel rides, and a lot more. There were very comfortable sitting and relaxing sofas, chairs and benches close to each entertainment area.

For dinner, we were seated in a large hall in a typical Rajasthan style, which is sitting on the floor with an individual low table for dining. Food was served in a large plate called Thalli. Dinner was authentic Rajasthan vegetarian cuisines consisting of dals, vegetables, and rice cooked into several dishes. One of the dishes was sweet rice with a ladle full of Ghee (butter fat) in the center of it. We liked some of the makai and bajra rotis, flat breads, and Rajasthni Mathaii (sweets). Some local people were enjoying these delicacies so much, they were eating quite fast. We being Panjabi were not used to Rajasthani taste. However, Mohinder tried all the dinner items and apparently enjoyed only a few. In India each region has its own authentic dishes which could be very different in taste due to ingredients and spices. The visit to Chokhi Dhani was seeing the cultural heritage of Rajasthan in a very short time.

The rest of the time in Jaipur was spent shopping. We bought some jewelry, clothes, shoes and bed spreads. The Jaipur trip was quite educational, interesting and a delightful experience. While living in India, we often discussed a visit to Pink City due to its history, culture and its unique beauty. A close friend of mine graduated from the Jaipur University and often talked about the city.

After Jaipur we came back to Delhi and got ready for our Panjab trip. We were so excited to enjoy meeting relatives in Panjab. It was like home coming. We flew from Delhi to Amritsar. At the Amritsar airport, we were warmly received by Mohinder's cousin, Rajiv Singh Arora. We came to Mohinder's maternal ancestral home, 10 Daswanda Singh Rd., presently the residence of Mohinder's maternal uncle,

S. Jagjit Singh Arora and his family. It was a grand reception by the family. There was so much excitement to receive Mohinder in good health and happy. It was a home coming celebration for Mohinder.

With Amritsar family.

After our family reunion and celebration, we visited Sri Harmandir Sahib to offer our humble prayers and thanks for all the blessings. It was a spiritual bliss that we felt from Sri Guru Ram Das Sahib Ji. We sat and listened to Kirtan from Sri Harmandir Sahib Ji. It was very joyous visit to the Sikh holiest city, Mohinder's birth place, our wedding city and our first home city as a young couple. There were so many very joyful memories of Sri Amritsar. It was a great feeling to be at Amritsar and visit our favorite places such as restaurants, stores and more.

We contacted all our relatives in Amritsar and scheduled visiting them. Most of them were Mohinder's first cousins.

With Mohan auntie and Nina at Sri Harmandir Sahib

Heart to heart talk

The next day we started visiting the rest of the relatives in Amritsar. We enjoyed their hospitality and exchanged stories of various events which took place during all those years since Mohinder had visited them last. Lots of things had happened during that time such as their children, like ours, were grown, married, settled and had their own children. There was so much to talk about and enjoy. We had so much fun sharing memorable old times. It was a great feeling and joyous reunion.

After having a great time at Amritsar, Mohinder and I took a taxi to my native village, Jande Sarai. My side of the family was anxiously waiting for us, especially Mohinder. They were so excited to welcome Mohinder. When Mohinder walked into our newly built ancestral home, she was pleasantly surprised and remarked, "I am so happy to see the little home with all kind of modern facilities." Mohinder saw the house for the first time. The home has three full baths with hot and cold running water and modern facilities with a kitchen. There are four bedrooms, two large living rooms, and a large hall on the top floor. The hall is an all-purpose room with a front porch which has a wonderful view of the village and the surroundings. All floors are white marble. Water is supplied by our well right in our court yard. When we four brothers decided to rebuild the home, Mohinder proposed that it should be a modern, comfortable home for us and our children to visit and stay in the village. We agreed and tried to do it accordingly.

In the living room with Dad's picture in the back ground

With sister- in-law, Jagir Kaur Sarai

We slept in our bedroom and enjoyed our breakfast the next day. My cousins invited us for lunch and dinner and treated us with the authentic local dishes such as Mikki- di - Rotti with Sag (fresh mustard tender stems and leaves with some other greens from our own fields). I took Mohinder around to see the rest of my family. We visited our Gurdwara Sahib, where I learned the value of faith in childhood and started my life journey.

From Jande Sarai, we went back to Amritsar to celebrate Diwali (famous festival of lights). Amritsar Diwali celebration is very special with lots of festivities, particularly at Sri Harmandir Sahib as Sri Guru Hargovind Sahib Ji (6th Sikh Guru) came back from Gwalior. It was quite a celebration after our living in Amritsar when we used to enjoy it every year. It brought back some unforgettable memories.

Two days after Diwali is Tikka (Bhai Dooj). We coordinated the trip for Mohinder to participate in the Tikka ceremony for Bhra Ji, S.Jagjit Singh Arora, with his sisters, Bhen Ji Balbir Kaur, and Mohan Auntie. Tikka signifies the sincerest prayers from sisters for the happy and long life of the brother. Sisters apply a ceremonial saffron mark with rice grain on the forehead of their brother and treat him with sweets and other delicacies including fruits such as Pomegranate, the brother in return blesses the sisters and give gifts, money and treats the whole family to a special meal. S. Jagjit Singh Arora took us out to a very good restaurant and treated us to Amritsar delicacies. It was just wonderful to celebrate the Tikka in Amritsar.

After Tikka and the memorable Amritsar visit with the great hospitality of S. Jagjit Singh Arora family, we were ready to visit Hoshiarpur and other places to meet other relatives. Bhen Ji arranged a taxi from Hoshiarpur to come to Amritsar to pick us up and take us to Hoshiarpur. Bhen Ji,

Mohinder and I went to Hoshiarpur, Mohinder's home. It was another homecoming. We were received by Bhen Ji's neighbors and very friendly families. They had a delicious dinner ready for us. It was a very pleasant home coming. Next morning, we were ready to walk around the neighborhood to enjoy memories of good old times such as my Panjab University College days and Mohinder's childhood, school and college times. I was reliving my college life while living in a little apartment next to Mohinder's home.

I remembered times with my friends, Baby and Lovely, and tutoring Mohinder and lot more. I walked around in the neighborhood to see all the favorite places such as my then apartment and some special shops and saw many people. A young man told me that Dar Ji's (my father-in-law) textile supervisor, S. Amolak Singh now in his nineties, was living next door. I was excited to see S. Amolak Singh. That young man was Amolak Singh's grandson. I visited Amolak Singh and enjoyed tea and snacks with him and talked about good old times. He had a great memory of times as employee of Dar Ji and Dar Ji's generosity as his employer. S. Amolak Singh was treated by Dar Ji as a friend and a family member.

Bhen Ji had kept the home well maintained, well - furnished and comfortable. We relived many unforgettable memories. I could feel the good old times we had shared.

With Bhen Ji in the back porch

In the Mohinder's parental living room

On the roof top

After having a great time at Hoshiarpur, we were ready to visit the rest of the relatives. Next we were to see my elder sister, Pritam Kaur Bajwa, in her village, Takkipur, which is close to Dasuya in the Hoshiarpur district, about 30 miles from Hoshiarpur. My brother, S. Pritam Singh, came in his car with his driver and took us to Takkipur. My sister was so excited to see us, especially Mohinder. Her hugs were so warm and full of love. She had a home cooked lunch waiting for us. We enjoyed the lunch and exchanged some gifts. Then she gave us a grand tour of her beautiful newly built home.

With sister and brother at Takkipur

She wanted us to stay with her overnight. However, we had to leave due to our tight schedule to get back to Panchkula before dark and spend some time with my brother's family before heading back to Bangkok.

We drove to Panchkula and enjoyed the welcome from my brother's family. They were so excited to see Mohinder. After a delicious dinner, we had a great visit and shared stories. It was quite late before we went to sleep. The next day we did some things in Chandigarh, such as shopping for clothing, shoes and spices, and enjoyed family company especially my brother's grandsons, Rekrit and Kremit. Kremit is a very intelligent young boy with very versatile knowledge. We became good friends in a short time with some mutual interests, like American wrestlers which Kremit knew a lot about.

We attended a function at Satluz Public School, founded by my brother. Presently he is serving as Director of the school. Mohinder and I were special guests at the function. It was quite a festivity with children's dances, singing and speeches from some dignitaries of Chandigarh and Panchkula. The function was followed by a party with delightful food. It was an interesting and enjoyable event.

My brother took us around to show us some historical places. One of those was a newly built Baba Banda Singh Bahadur memorial at Chapper Cheri, a village close to Sahibzada Ajit Singh (SAS) Nagar, Mohali a suburb of Chandigarh. This memorial has a great significance in the Sikh History. At this site in May 1710, the Sikh army under the command of Baba Banda Singh Bahadur, a great Sikh warrior, defeated the Mughal army commanded by Wazir Khan, the governor of Sirhind. Wazir Khan, along with some other important Muslim rulers of Panjab region, were killed in this battle. It brought back some very important events from the Sikh history, especially the martyrdom of four sons (Sahibzadas) of Sri Guru Govind Singh Ji and his mother Mata Gujri Ji.

At Chapper Chiri memorial

At this site there stands a 328 ft. tall Fateh Burj, meaning Victory Tower, in the center of the battle field. It is one of the tallest towers in India.

At Victory Tower

Wazir Khan was an unjust and bitter enemy of Sri Guru Govind Singh Ji, tenth Sikh Guru. Along with the Hilly Rajas and Mughal army forces, he waged several battles against Sri Guru Govind Singh Ji, including the battle of Chamkaur Sahib, however he did not win any. In the Chamkaur Sahib battle Guru Sahib, his two elder sons, Sahibzada Ajit Singh Ji (18 years), Sahibzada Jujhar Singh Ji (16 years) and forty Singhs fought bravely against 100,000 enemy forces. Both Sahibzadas, three of the Panj Piarey and 26 Singhs were martyred. Guru Sahib was asked by five

Singhs, including two of the Panj Piarey, to leave the Chamkaur Sahib fortress. Guru Sahib, obeying the order, left the battle field with three Singhs including two Panj Piarey (Bhai Dya Singh Ji and Bhai Dharam Singh Ji) only after challenging the enemy army with three loud challenge calls, "Peer of India (Guru Govind Singh) is leaving." Seven Singhs were left behind in the fortress who fought valiantly the next day and achieved martyrdoms. This battle was, historically, a unique battle of righteousness, fought by a small number of Singh Warriors under the command of Sri Guru Govind Singh Ji against a large army of the unjust Mughal Empire.

Furthermore, Wazir Khan had martyred two very young Sahibzadas of Sri Guru Govind Singh Ji, Baba Jorawar Singh Ji and Baba Fateh Singh Ji, along with Mata Gujri Ji, Guru Sahib's mother. The Sahibzadas were only nine and six years old respectively. It was because they refused to bow to Wazir Khan and to accept Islam. They were bricked alive at Sirhind. This chilling, terrible event infuriated Sikhs, Hindus and even some Muslim rulers of Panjab.

Sri Guru Govind Singh Ji had already weakened the Mughal Empire through various battles and by creating the Khalsa Panth. The victory of Chapper Chiri battle further shook the roots of the Mughal Empire significantly and encouraged the other regions of India to revolt against the unjust, cruel tyrant Mughal Emperor for the freedom of India from the Mughal Empire.

After this battle, Baba Banda Singh Bahadur established the first Sikh Rule in Panjab with a secular and just rule, for all people regardless of their faith and caste, based on the Sikh principles. Later in 1799, Maharaja Ranjit Singh, Sher- e- Panjab (lion of Panjab), established the great Khalsa/Sikh Empire which extended from Khyber Pass in the West to Tibet in the East, from Kashmir in the North to Mithankot in the South. It included present day Pakistan, Panjab, Haryana, Himachal Pradesh, Jammu and Kashmir. The area of the empire was 100,436 sq. miles. Maharaja Ranjit Singh was a brave warrior, just, secular, humble and a firm believer in Sikh principles. He abolished death sentence in his kingdom. He passed on in 1839 at the age of 58. The Khalsa Empire existed from 1799 to 1849 before it was taken by the British Empire. After two divisions, first by the British Empire in 1947 and second by the Indian Government, present day Panjab area is only 19,445 sq. miles.

The visit to Chapper Chiri Memorial was an important lesson in Sikh history. It was exalting to be standing at this site and realizing the victorious Sikh warriors fighting a great battle serving justice to tyrants like Wazir Khan and freeing India from the Mughal Empire.

After having a great time in Panjab while visiting all the relatives, friends and places, we thanked my brother and family for all their hospitality and taking us around for shopping and sightseeing. With heavy hearts and tearful eyes, we hugged my brother and his family and waved good bye.

With brother and family

We took a taxi to Delhi to fly back to Bangkok. In Delhi we stayed with S. Tejinder Singh Arora. Mohinder was to apply Tikka to Tejinder as the last important event before leaving India. Tejinder being the first boy and Mohinder being the oldest girl on the maternal side, are almost of the same age. Tejinder was always represented as the oldest brother of Mohinder's brothers. She had been waiting for this occasion for years as she had been sending Tikka to Tejinder by mail. This year it was the real thing although belated by a week or so. Both enjoyed the Tikka ceremony very much and there was visible excitement at the ceremony. There was an exchange of gifts and a delicious ceremonial lunch afterward. It was a wonderful way to complete the Indian trip which turned out to be even better than expected.

With Tejinder at Tikka

Tejinder Singh drove us to the Delhi Airport. Again another emotional farewell hugging Tejinder and family, we left India and flew back to Bangkok, Thailand. It was one of the best trips to India with so many unforgettable memories. Nina and Sukhdev received us at the Bangkok airport. Nina looked at me and commented, "Dad, you don't look good." I had a cough, an ache on my left side and a little breathing difficulty. After reaching home, she checked me and diagnosed that my left lung did not sound normal and I had Pneumonia.

In the morning she took me to the Bangkok Hospital and I was diagnosed with a severe case of Pneumonia with fluids around the lower part of my left lung for which I needed immediate surgery. Nina being a doctor in the same hospital, got my surgery scheduled the same afternoon. I was in surgery for about 5 hours and had Mohinder and the rest of the family worried about my health. When I came out of the recovery room, and saw the family very worried and surprised to see me after such a long surgery. Nina had assured them that I was in good hands and going to be all right. Drs. were surprised that I was travelling and having fun in India while having such a serious health problem.

Nina secured my private room on the top floor of the hospital with a window, a beautiful view of Bangkok, and the nursing station across from my room. Two drain tubes were coming out of my left side to drain the fluids from around the left lung. I was given exceptional care in the hospital. The surgeon and the attending Doctor had done an excellent job taking care of my problem. Nurses used to call me "Papa". They said, "Papa call us any time for any help." I was treated like royalty which made my hospital stay quite comfortable. Mohinder was still quite worried. She visited me with family members every day, brought home cooked food and stayed with me most of the time. Several times, she stayed with me overnight although I assured her that I was in excellent hands. I was in the Hospital for about 10 days until the surgery wounds were healed and the fluids were drained before I was discharged. I was not allowed to travel back to America for about four weeks until the Drs. were satisfied with my recovery. Everybody treated me so well that I felt spoiled by the tender loving care. During my recovery, Nina took a week off from work and took us to Elephant Head beach in Thailand along with her family for some restful time.

By now, I felt good about traveling back to America. We flew back in Jan 2013. Our family received us at the Asheville Airport and were so happy to see me healthy. We felt so good to be back home after about three months of traveling. Within a few days, Sumandeep scheduled an appointment with my doctor to check my healing progress from the operation. My doctor was waiting for me as he knew what I went through in Bangkok.

The Dr. checked me thoroughly and ordered further lab tests including an MRI to be sure that my lungs and healing were satisfactory. All the tests came out normal. This good news made the family happy and relieved from the worry about my health. We resumed our normal life and activities. Mohinder was playing tennis regularly, even subbing at times.

Arjun Singh's Turban Tying

In Jan 2014, we were back in Bangkok, this time to participate in the Turban Tying ceremony of our grandson, Arjun Singh (Nina's son), who was almost fifteen. It is a very important occasion indicating that the youngster is not a child anymore. We were so excited, especially Mohinder, to be part of this ceremony. We reached Bangkok on Jan 9 as the ceremony was on Jan 10. The event was at Singh Sabha Bangkok Gurdwara Sahib in the presence of Sri Guru Granth Sahib Ji with Kirtan and Ardas (prayer) by Bhai Ji, a Sikh preacher. There were family members, relatives and friends partaking in the ceremony. It was very exciting to see Arjun with a beautiful nicely tied red turban on his head.

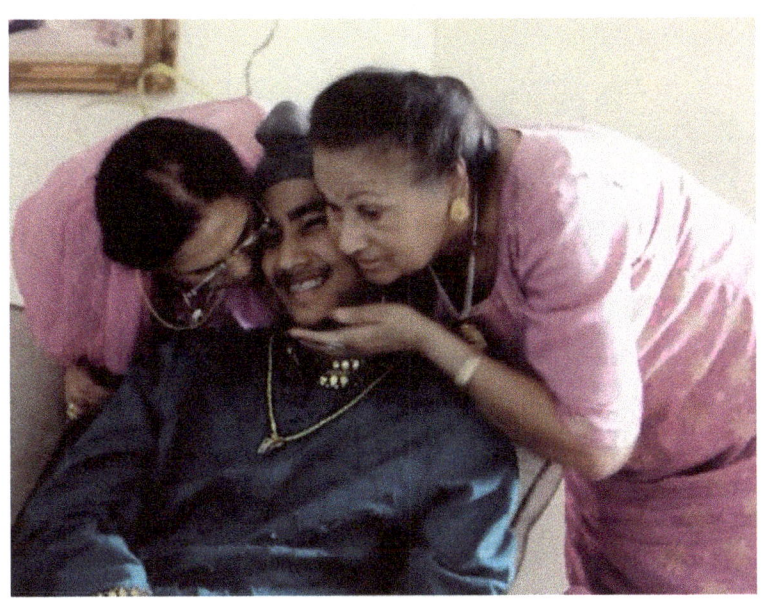

Hug from both Grand mamas

Arjun with Turban

Vietnam Trip

After Arjun Singh's Turban celebration, Nina told us, "Next week you are going to Vietnam to have some romantic time together." It was a surprise for us to spend about a week in Vietnam. She had booked tour tickets of Hanoi and Halong Bay in Vietnam. We were to stay in Sofitel Metropole in Hanoi and on a small luxury ship in Halong Bay. We were thrilled to see Vietnam, a country which first fought the French for freedom from French Rule, and then the well-known war in the sixties with South Vietnam, being helped by the United States of America. South Vietnam was fighting to be independent from the communist rule of North Vietnam.

We landed in Hanoi, the capital of Vietnam, and as expected the Sofitel Metropole Hotel van was waiting for us outside the airport. We reached the hotel after a nice ride through the country side and the city. We enjoyed the ride and saw the natives riding bicycles carrying big loads of various articles such as flowers and household items.

The Sofitel Metropole is almost in the center of Hanoi, close to Hoan Kiem Lake in the Hoan Kiem business district, the commercial center of Hanoi. Hoan Kiem Lake, the lake of restored sword, is the home of Hanoi's giant turtle. The lake has the Turtle Tower on a small island in the center. On the north side, there is Jade Island with Jade Temple which is connected to the shore by a red wooden bridge. The lake has a beautiful sidewalk around it with flower beds and flower pots, and shrubs decorating it everywhere. There are benches for resting and enjoying the beauty of the place. There were all kinds of activities such as painting, exercising, jogging and picnicking. We walked around the lake and had our lunch there and enjoyed the beauty. It is a scenic spot in Hanoi; therefore, one of the tourist attractions.

At Hoan Kiem Lake

There were some very good restaurants and bakeries along the lake sidewalk. These restaurants were popular places for tourists to eat. A friend of ours recommended one which served delicious local and American dishes. It was our favorite eating place in Hanoi. Outside of the lake is the road and all kind of stores for shopping.

People were generally cheerful, friendly and helpful. There were only a few traffic lights and pedestrian crossings around the lake road; therefore, it was a little tricky to cross it in between moving vehicles. While we were waiting to cross the road, a young couple came along. The young lady held Mohinder's hand and the gentleman held mine and we crossed the road by holding hands. We thanked them and they gave us a big smile with "You're Welcome." We were surprised at the incident and moved by the helpful nature of the Vietnamese people. We enjoyed walking on the sidewalks and purchased some snacks from street vendors. The shopping was fun around the hotel. We had a memorable time in the historic city of Hanoi and learned a lot about its history.

Now we were ready to go to Halong Bay, meaning 'a lonely planet.' We were picked up by the hotel van and drove through the countryside for about four hours to reach the bay. After reaching the bay, a boat took us to our ship. We checked into our cabin which was luxurious with a window, and a beautiful view of the bay. After relaxing and getting ready, we were given the grand tour of the ship to get familiar with all the facilities such as the dining hall, entertainment facilities, and the top deck. The dining hall had delightful food and great service. The top deck was an inviting place to spend the evenings and have some drinks. There we made some good friends and exchanged our contact information with a few couples. We were given the schedule of the whole tour by the ship staff to enjoy our stay and be ready for the activities.

The bay lies on Vietnam's Northeastern coast, and is unique, with emerald color waters and thousands of towering limestone islands covered with rainforest trees and vegetation. It is home to three traditional floating villages with 400 homes and about 2,000 population. Each community is complete with a school, post office and a temple. We took a village tour and learned a lot about these interesting people. Our package included the tour of the fishing village, Sung Sot Cave (surprise cave) and Soi Sim Island.

The fishing village tour was in a row boat, with a smiling young lady rowing the boat and giving us the grand tour of the village. She was very adept at explaining the various parts of the village, such as the school, post office and the temple, and the villagers busy in their various daily activities. There were small boats filled with items for the villagers. These were like floating shops, fulfilling the daily needs of the floating households.

Fishing Village

Temple at the fishing village

Our tour lady was so nice, that I wanted to give her a ten US dollar gratuity. I asked Mohinder about it. Mohinder said, "Give her at least 20 dollars." I said, "I don't have the change." Mohinder said, "Give her 10 dollars and rest in Thai Bahts and Vietnamese money." I smiled and gave our guide the money. She was quite happy and we were too. It was impressive to have the tour of the fishing village.

These people live in floating wooden houses. Each house is a complete household with various rooms for living, cooking and entertainment like watching TV. They even had pet dogs and cats. It was amazing to see their life style which is a unique way of living and maintaining essential Vietnamese Traditions. The livelihood of these interesting people is mainly fishing and aquiculture supplemented by giving tours. Mohinder was so impressed by these unique people that she commented, "It is amazing to see these people so contented and happy with such relatively limited resources."

Next we had the tour of the surprise cave. After a narrow entry and a few steps into the cave, it became bigger and a giant, airy and spectacular cave opened up with a large theater, and several other chambers with beautiful ceilings and colorful chandeliers formed by stalactites. The floor was formed with rocks of diverse shapes. We were mystified by its beauty and size (130,000 square ft. area). It is a one of a kind amazingly beautiful natural wonder. We never saw such a big and beautiful cave before.

In the surprise cave

To have some fun at the beach, we visited Soi Sim Island in the bay. This island has a picturesque beach and food stalls, chairs and tables to have a picnic on the beach. Furthermore, it has a view tower with several hundred steps to the top. We climbed only half of the way and it was high enough to have the scenic view of the bay without getting tired.

At the beach

On the view tower

We enjoyed the stay at Halong Bay and had a great time. Now we were ready to go back to Hanoi. Our van started back in the late morning. On the way, we saw villagers working in the rice paddies and fields with the

Vietnamese traditional bamboo or straw cone hats. They are a hardworking happy people. Half way to Hanoi, our van stopped at a rest area with a shopping center and restaurants for lunch. There was an interesting art studio where artists were working and selling their work. It was a great place for Mohinder, the artist, to spend time. She talked to the artists and learned about the Vietnamese art techniques.

In a Vietnam art studio

We reached Hanoi in the evening with enough time to enjoy doing some shopping and an after dinner walk on the street. The next day we left Hanoi with an excellent feeling about our Vietnam trip. We learned a lot about the country, which fought two long wars and is now doing quite well.

After our Vietnam trip and having some relaxing time with the family, Nina had planned a trip to Halong

Beach. Halong Beach is a scenic beach with luxurious resorts. We stayed in a hotel with beautiful sandy beach, big swimming pool, and restaurants next to the ocean. It was another fun and relaxing place. One of Mohinder's favorite natural attractions is the ocean's view.

Enjoying the beach scene

Mohan auntie and Mohinder at the beach.

After spending a great time of five weeks in Thailand and Vietnam, we were ready to come home. We flew back to Asheville, and were received by the family welcoming us home as we were missed a lot.

We traveled a lot more after retirement, but these few bigger trips were more exciting, with so many unforgettable memories.

Chapter 13

MOHINDER AND ESHA'S COLLEGE EDUCATION

Our granddaughter, Esha, graduated from Carolina Day School in May 2009. In school she majored in French and music. She was interested in pursuing these two fields in college. She applied for undergraduate study in several colleges. Two universities, the University of Washington, Seattle and the University of North Carolina, Greensboro (UNCG) accepted her with financial aid. UNCG later gave her full financial aid, and being close to home, was a better choice. Esha decided to go to UNCG which is one of the best schools for music. We were very happy with her choice.

She started her university studies in the fall of 2009 and was in constant contact with us through phone and frequent visits by her or by us. Mohinder and Esha were on the phone almost daily to stay in touch. They were best friends. Esha sought Nanima's (grandmother) guidance all the time and Mohinder loved it. Esha was doing very well in college and her studies were progressing excellently. Esha spent one semester in France and one in New Zealand for her bachelor degree. She finished her undergraduate work and was excited to be a college graduate. She managed money so well that at the end of her college, instead of loans, she had saved a couple thousand dollars. It was amazing. Now we all were looking forward to her graduation. Her graduation took place on May 10, 2013.

Esha's graduation was another big event to celebrate. The whole family went to Greensboro to attend the event. Esha graduated with bachelor degrees in Music and French with honors. She won quite a few awards and was quite popular both in her class and with the university staff. Esha's Professors were impressed with her achievements and her cheerful personality. She made us very proud. Mohinder was beaming with happiness to see her oldest granddaughter graduated from college with excellent accomplishments. Esha had been a role model for her younger six cousins. They are following in her foot steps and doing great in several fields. We are anxiously awaiting their graduations as well.

Esha, Proud Graduate

Esha, Bina and proud Nanima.

After Esha's graduation, it was Mother's Day, a time to honor Mohinder as a wonderful mother for which Sumandeep took us to the Biltmore Forest Country Club for dinner. It is a wonderful place in Asheville to celebrate such special occasions. All the mothers from our side of the family and Sumandeep's in-laws were treated to a great dinner and gathering of the family members. Within a few days, it was Mohinder's 74th birthday, another occasion to celebrate. We had a wonderful birthday party with dinner, cake and more.

Soon after graduation, Esha was contacted, perhaps due to her achievements, by the University of North Carolina Chapel Hill to apply for a Transatlantic Master degree (TAM). This program is popularly known as a degree without borders. Besides studying at the Chapel Hill campus, a portion is completed overseas at a European University.

Students learn about European Institutions and issues such as security, immigration and economic disparity. Esha's Europe study was to be at the Bremen University, Germany. Esha was excited to start her graduate study. We all, especially Mohinder, were so proud of Esha.

Esha was accepted in TAM with a 10,000 dollar scholarship. She was to start her master's program in the fall of 2013. Mohinder was so happy with Esha's educational progress. In August 2013, Esha moved to Chapel Hill to start her graduate study. Mohinder helped her move and get settled in Chapel Hill. Esha found a nice apartment close to the University campus and Mohinder wanted to see it before her moving in. Mohinder always wanted to make sure that the location and security of a place was satisfactory. Mohinder and Esha furnished it nicely. Before long Esha was quite popular at the campus. She started working at the campus radio station. Her professors were very happy with her grades and furthermore with her extracurricular activities and pleasant personality. Moreover to have some extra money, she started part-time work at a coffee shop. She was quite happy at Chapel Hill.

In the meantime, Esha applied for a Critical Language Scholarship (CLS) in Panjabi. CLS is a fully funded summer overseas language and cultural immersion program of the US State Department. Esha was awarded the scholarship for which she was to spend two summer months in 2014 to study Panjabi at Chandigarh, Panjab, India. It was an unbelievable opportunity for a person with Panjabi as her ancestral language. She had learned some Panjabi through classes at Midwest Gurdwara Sahib in Kansas City. We, including relatives in Panjab, were so excited about this unique opportunity.

Esha was ready to go to Panjab and then to Bremen and graduate with her TAM degree. God willing, she was lined up to graduate in May 2015. We were anxiously waiting for that important day.

Reoccurrence of Cancer

Mohinder visited her Oncologist for a routine checkup. Her doctor found some markers in the blood test that were not normal. He ordered lab screening tests to be sure that everything was OK. Shockingly, Mohinder's cancer had reoccurred, this time in her liver. Hearing this, Nina came from Bangkok and joined the family to decide on her treatment. We consulted various well-known Oncologists in the region for the next step. The best possible treatment was started within a short time with prayers. Luckily, Mohinder responded better than expected to the treatment and the lesions were shrinking quite rapidly. One oncologist remarked that we found a winning horse. It was great news. Mohinder, during the treatment, was an exemplary person enjoying her tennis and other activities.

To celebrate the good news about Mohinder's health and our 54th wedding anniversary, we went to a beach in Charleston SC for a week to have fun in the historic city. Esha arranged the trip and booked the stay for four of us (Mohinder, Bina, Esha and I) at a beachfront Hotel: the Tides, Folly Beach SC. Sumandeep had booked an anniversary dinner in a famous restaurant in Charleston and Esha was in charge of other meals. Esha knew the town well and took us to a good French and other restaurants for our favorite foods. It was a very enjoyable celebration week at the beach.

Got a Pet Dog

We had been thinking of getting a small pet dog and were not certain about the breed. Our neighbor, across the street, had four white little Westie dogs. Mohinder talked to the neighbor and came to know that the Westie, West

Highland Terrier, are one of the best pet dogs. Mohinder said, "How about a Westie Puppy." We all agreed and started looking for a Westie. In August 2013 Nina found a Westie breeder online who was only about four miles from us. He had four, eight week old, female puppies. Mohinder, Sumandeep, Nina and I went to see them and one of the puppies picked us, rather than our picking her. She was so cute, happy and loving. We brought her home and named her Lilly due to her white color. She loved everyone in the family and Mohinder in particular. She became Mohinder's pet. Mohinder got an invisible electric fence around the house so that Lilly could run around in the yard freely without getting lost. Mohinder housetrained her and taught her to ring the bell (hanging from the door knob) whenever she needed to go out. She is so well trained that she never messed in the house. Mohinder taught her dog tricks and often played with her. Lilly turned out to be a lovely pet. She obeyed Mohinder, while sometimes ignored us. Mohinder became her master, and often had Lilly in her lap and loved it.

With Lilly

Lilly is full of energy and always on the lookout for a good time such as playing or going out for a walk. She is very friendly, happy and of lively nature. She loves to dig, particularly if there is a mole tunneling in the yard. We had mole problem in the yard before Lilly came. Lilly got rid of them. Lilly is very popular in the neighborhood. All our neighbors know Lilly and often stop to say hello to her when we are walking.

Chapter 14
MOHINDER'S 75TH BIRTHDAY PARTY

Another milestone in Mohinder's age, the 75th birthday on May14, had approached and the whole family was excited to do something special for her. A grand birthday party, on Aug.16, 2014, was planned by our daughters in addition to the usual celebration by the family on May 14, 2014. August 16 suited all the family members including our grandchildren. Esha was to be in Panjab from June- August on her Panjabi Scholarship study. She was to come back on August 14. She wouldn't want to miss her Ninama's birthday party. For the party, the Hilton Hotel Biltmore Park Town Square, specifically its Pisgah ballroom, was selected. This hotel is walking distance from our home and thus very convenient.

Mother's Day was only a few days before her birthday; therefore, the celebration started with a Mother's Day dinner at the Biltmore Forest Country Club with the whole family. On May 14, Sumandeep had a birthday party at her home with cake, dinner and all. To surprise Mohinder, all her friends, especially her tennis partners, were invited. Mohinder was pleasantly surprised to see all her friends singing "Happy Birthday to you." She got emotional and commented that this was a very special birthday celebration. She deserved it as she had been such an exemplary and caring mother and grandmother. Then there was another surprise dinner in a special downtown Asheville restaurant. After all these festivities, the plans for the August 16th party were started.

With her Tennis Friends

For that, we visited the hotel once again and checked the party room, the Pisgah Ballroom. It was large enough to accommodate 70 plus people, the expected number of guests. Then invitations were sent to all the relatives (both sides of the family) and friends. They RSVP'd indicating that most of them were excited to grace the occasion. Once we knew the approximate number of guests coming to the party, the menu was the next item on the list. Sumandeep and Mohinder took charge of the menu. We visited the hotel and met with the lady in charge of the party arrangements. After discussing the food with the lady, we met the Head Chef. He was a delightful person and familiar with most of the dishes (some Panjabi such as lamb curry and Palak (spinach) Paneer) on the menu. He suggested preparing all the items on the menu and invited us to come and taste them. We made a reservation to have dinner at the Hilton. We tasted all the menu items and Mohinder suggested some changes to make the Indian dishes more authentic. The Chef, being open minded, agreed to make the changes and invited us again to dinner. We went the second time and tasted the food which we approved. Mohinder thanked the Chef for the job well done. The Chef was happy and was excited to serve his dishes at the party.

After finalizing the menu, we were ready to think about the rest of the party preparations such as decorations, music, and a slide show. Bina and Esha took the responsibility of the decorations for the party ballroom; Nina and her daughter, Anya, offered to prepare a photo book of Mohinder and a slide show; Esha took the role as master of ceremonies (MC); the whole family offered to assist them as needed. It was a well-coordinated team effort to have fun at this special occasion. Mohinder was an advisor and supervisor in general for all the preparations. Plans were getting better and better as the Aug 16 date was approaching.

On party day, the Pisgah Ballroom was beautifully decorated with a sign, "HAPPY 75th BIRTHDAY", balloons and ribbons. The long wall was used to project pictures from Mohinder's picture book. The book was placed close to the door for guests to see Mohinder's life in pictures, and for them to add their comments and signing. All the family members, especially seven of our grandchildren were working, excited to make the party a success. Their Nanima was beaming with happiness to see all the preparations.

Guests started coming in at 6PM and in about half an hour, most of them had arrived. Mohinder could not believe her eyes seeing most of the family members (four siblings, Mama and S. Avtar Singh Arora Mohinder's favorite maternal uncle) from her side of the family and their families; my two brothers and sister with their families; our daughters, grandchildren, son-in- laws and Sumandeep's in-laws; Mohinder's Tennis friends and their husbands; and our friends from Asheville. It was exciting to see them all at this special occasion.

The party started with finger foods, refreshments and drinks (soft drinks, champagne and other wines) from the bar. It was a mingling time and happy hour. It was fun to see every one having a good time. After that, guests were seated in their designated seats on well-arranged tables with lots of room for other activities and dancing. It was a buffet dinner with tables for salad, appetizers, main course dishes and desserts. Esha, MC, was busy with the entertainment during the dinner, music and the slide show which started with Mohinder's childhood and continued into her youth and married life including children and grandchildren. It was a brief history of Mohinder's life represented in slides. Mohinder could not believe all of this. After that there were speeches and songs, mainly by Mohinder's family members.
S. Avtar Singh Arora sang one of Mohinder's favorite movie songs which was so good that Mohinder and some of us started singing with him. After dinner there was dancing. Esha had a very good selection of Bhangra Songs and more. Our granddaughters and other relatives were dancing and having a great time, especially the little children who stole the show.

In the meantime, dessert and coffee were served. Close to the end of the party, Mohinder cut the Birthday Cake and everybody enjoyed a piece of it. The party was flawless and memorable, about four hours long - an event in which everyone had a great time.

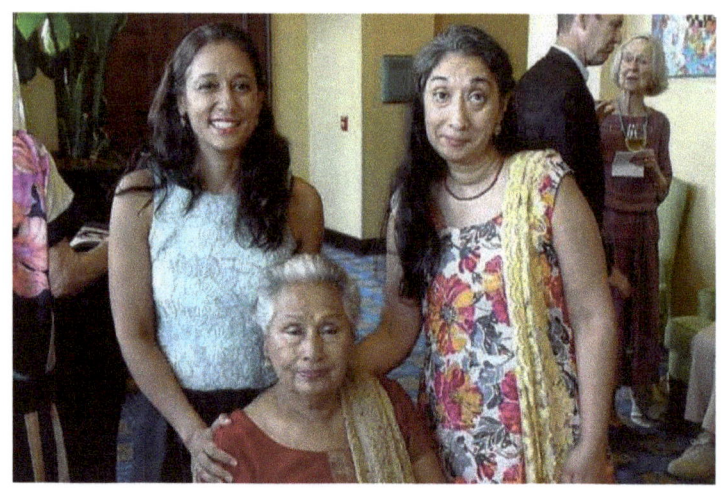

The Birthday Party

The next day our relatives from out of town came over to say goodbye before leaving. Our daughters and granddaughters had tea and breakfast ready for them. Mohinder had a paper bag with food and fruit ready for each family for their journey home. There were emotional hugs and goodbyes as they left. Later on, the party was talked about a lot.

Soon after the party, Mohinder and Bina planned to go to New York with Esha to see her off to Bremen, Germany for her TAM study. Three of them, best friends, had a good time in New York.

Esha worked hard in Bremen to learn German, and to communicate with Panjabi immigrants settled in Germany. She completed all the requirements, course work and research work. Besides her studies, she made good friends and enjoyed German hospitality at Christmas time. Almost every day Esha and her Nanima were communicating by phone or facetiming. We, especially Mohinder, were anxiously waiting for Esha's return from Germany, with her Master in Political Science.

Besides studies, Esha was required to do an internship for the graduation. While in Germany, she contacted Voice of America, USA (VOA) in Washington DC for the internship. She was accepted by VOA for a two month internship in the French section. She worked at VOA from March-May, 2015. She impressed her supervising staff to the point that they indicated Esha a possible job offer after her graduation. Esha graduated from the University of North Carolina Chapel Hill in May 2015. Her Nanima was so proud of Esha and her fast track educational successes. Mohinder hugged Esha and kissed her to show her excitement. When Esha said "VOA may hire me", all of us were so happy to hear that and were waiting for the job offer. Esha was enjoying home cooking and family.

Chapter 15

EXEMPLARY PERSON

Examples from Mohinder's life prove again and again that she had multiple admirable qualities in a single person. She was an exemplary daughter, sister, wife, mother, grandmother, friend, teacher, Sikh and a person in general.

Daughter

Being the first child in her family, she was loved and in return she was very obedient and respectful to her parents, grandparents and all other elderly members of the family. Her personality and manners earned their love and care.

Sister (Mohinder Ji Ji/Di Di)

She was a role model for her brothers, sisters and cousins. They loved her and sought her opinion in important matters in their lives. She was such a sincere and honest person and for that they respected her and her advice. Mohinder did not talk much; therefore, any secret was safe with her. Furthermore, she cared for her siblings and felt that she needed to help them in any and every way she could.

She was so thankful to God to see all the relatives from both sides of the family settled and doing well in America. She loved to prepare Thanksgiving, Christmas and 4th of July dinners for the whole family, including a number of extended family members. Sometimes on these occasions, she would host as many as 40 family members, all having a great time.

Wife

I knew Mohinder for 60 years, first for two years as an acquaintance through tutoring her, the next two years as her betrothed and then for 56 years as my beloved wife. I always felt blessed and fortunate to have Mohinder as my life partner. She was a loving, understanding, caring and sharing wife. She taught me to see some situations in a realistic way rather than being naïve which helped me a lot. We enjoyed every moment of our married life. Whenever we had a difference of opinion, we worked it out as soon as possible and did not let it go even to the next day. We lived with one principle: Enjoy every moment of life to the maximum; however, within our means and not with borrowed money. We always felt rich at heart, even when we did not necessarily feel it with the bank balance. Thanks to God, we were always blessed with enough.

Mother

Mohinder enjoyed raising our three daughters the best possible way as a loving and caring mother. She had an amazing motherly instinct which to me was the sixth sense. She knew exactly whenever any one of them was sick or in trouble. We could not hide anything from her as she, seemingly, could read our minds.

Furthermore, she always got the children involved in social and extracurricular activities such as participating in school sports, dramas and debates, etc. They were members of clubs such as 4H and girl scouts. They took dancing lessons and were involved in the city children's functions. For the spiritual aspect, they attended Gurdwara Services (Sat Sangs) and participated in children's activities such as learning the Panjabi Language, Gurbani and taking part in contests.

We wanted our children to be successful professionally and socially. Our number one priority was always our children and their proper growing up. As a family we had lots of fun times through vacationing and travels to supplement our routine daily life. All our family decisions were mutual as a team. Every member was given equal right.

It helped the whole family a lot. There were no secrets among us.

As desired, our children grew up exceptionally well. Sumandeep and Nina became medical Doctors, each at age twenty four. Bina became a Certified Nursing Assistant (CNA) and an artist. They are very happy, caring and loving daughters. We are so proud of them and feel blessed to have such a compassionate family.

Sikh

Mohinder, being born in Amritsar and in a very dedicated Sikh family, had a strong foundation to follow the Sikh Faith in the real sense. Sikhism is based on Gurbani, the text of Sri Guru Granth Sahib Ji; therefore, its correct interpretation is very important to follow the Sikh Faith properly. Dar Ji (Mohinder's dad) was one of the best interpreters of Gurbani I have ever known. He emphasized the correct pronunciation of Gurbani for its true understanding.

Mohinder practiced Sikhism by living the Sikh way of life and observing the Sikh principles: Earn your living honestly (Karat Karoo), share with others (Vand Chakoo), and meditate on the name of God (Namm Japo), always have a positive attitude (Chardi Kala), do selfless service for others (Sewa) and accept God's Will (Hukam) happily as all and everything is happening according to His Will. The ultimate goal of a Sikh is to have the soul emerge in God (Mukti) through deeds and service in this life. Human life is an opportunity, accomplished after numerous reincarnations, to achieve this goal. One way to achieve the Goal is to remember God whole-heatedly close to the end of this present life. After this achievement there wouldn't be any further reincarnations of the soul.

I often saw Mohinder sitting on the bed and meditating early in the morning. We often talked about Gurbani during our evening walks and in the mornings while listening to Gurbani Kirtan from Sri Harmandir Sahib Ji on the TV. Through these conversations, we tried to have a better understanding of Gurbani and practice it as intended. From all this information, Mohinder became a true and practical Sikh. Mohinder's realistic approach to all aspects of life kept her enjoying life to the best imaginable way under all circumstances.

In Nov 2014, one of her best friends from College, Manjit Bajwa- Virk and her husband came to visit us. Mohinder was so excited to see Manjit. Mohinder and Manjit being Artists visited most of the important Art Galleries in Asheville. We showed them Asheville and surrounding attractions such as the Blue Ridge Parkway and waterfalls.

With Manjit on the Blue Ridge Parkway

They caught up with lost time by sharing family stories and retired life activities, and had a great time together. Soon after their visit, on Nov 14, 2014, we attended the wedding of one of Mohinder's nieces in Kansas City and had a wonderful visit with our brothers, sisters, nephews and nieces in Kansas City.

With Sumandeep and Malvinder

It was also Tikka festival time, and for that Arvinderpal Singh arranged the Tikka celebration at his residence in which Mohinder, Malvinder, Harinderpal Singh and their families participated. It was an exciting event after several years of Mohinder sending Tikka by mail.

At Tikka with Arvinderpal and Harinderpal

In Jan 2015 as usual, we went to Bangkok to enjoy time with Nina and her family. For a week we went to a beach in Phuket. While lying on the beach, Mohinder accidently had her foot stepped on by a horse. Nina being with us, got Mohinder treated at a nearby hospital. Although Mohinder had a painful foot, it did not stop her from enjoying the fun at beach, one of her favorite places.

Furthermore, we visited Ayudhya/ Ayutthaya, a city about an hour drive from Bangkok. The modern city is close by the historical Park. The ruins of the old capital of Siam/Thailand are preserved beautifully as Ayudhya Historical Park. This park is recognized by UNESCO as one of the world's heritage centers. The park shows the splendors of the ancient Thai kingdom. Ayudhya was the capital of the Thai Kingdom from 1351-1767. During that period, it was an important trade center among Asian and some European countries. This city was described as one of the biggest and wealthiest cities in the East. The city is at the junction of two rivers.

It was interesting, and another lesson in history to see the various parts of the ancient city with excellent structures and Buddha sculptures. In addition, this name is the same as Ayudhya in Uttar Pradesh, India the birthplace of Lord Rama (Ram Chander Ji). Rama has also been used as a title by the Thai kings. Although the state religion is Buddhism, seemingly they believed in the Lord Rama's philosophy as well.

In Ayudhya

While we were in Thailand, my brothers, Jarnail Singh, Karnail Singh and sister-in-law Manjit (Jarnail Singh's wife) came to Bangkok. Nina was so excited to see her uncles and auntie visiting her for the first time in Thailand. Nina planned to show them around, scheduling time for massage and shopping. We had a great time with them while sightseeing, visiting old palaces and river side restaurants. The ladies as expected, enjoyed shopping, especially, the jewelry. It was a good week.

After having great time in Thailand, we came back to Asheville and resumed our normal activities. Mohinder was regularly playing tennis and having fun with her friends. All was going well and plans to celebrate Mother's Day and Mohinder's 76th birthday were under way. Esha was almost done with the internship with VOA and was ready to graduate from the University of North Carolina at Chapel Hill in May 2015. Furthermore, her plans were to stay home and enjoy time with the family before looking for a job. Mohinder was very excited about all this. It was a great feeling to see our oldest granddaughter, and Mohinder's best friend, graduating from the University.

Mohinder was visiting her oncologist regularly and her tests were satisfactory. Early in May 2015 there were indicators that Mohinder's treatment was not working; therefore, there was the need to change her treatment. Nina came from Thailand, and our family consulted oncologists for the next best step. One very promising option was for Mohinder to participate in a trial study which was conducted in Asheville by her oncologist. Mohinder started the new treatment and the results were optimistic.

Mohinder was keeping up with her tennis and other activities. The whole family joined a Tai Chi class. It was fun to have dance like slow motion exercises. Mohinder enjoyed seeing me having fun and messing up some of the steps. Her precious smile made me have more fun in the class. I never took sports and exercises seriously. After the class the whole family used to have lunch at some of our favorite restaurants in Asheville.

Mohinder's oncologist checked the results of the trial treatment and found that the results were not as good as expected; therefore, Mohinder needed to have chemo treatment. Everyone agreed and Mohinder started her chemo therapy. Mohinder's attitude was very optimistic, the oncologist said that after the treatment Mohinder should be back to normal after a short time. It was very good to know. Mohinder was playing tennis and was enjoying life to the fullest during the treatment.

Esha came back from Washington DC to attend her Master's graduation at UNC Chapel Hill. We were excited to see Esha. Mohinder's bear-hug was something else. Mohinder and Esha talked a long time to catch up with all that happened during the time they were separated. We were enjoying the reunion. There was a celebration of Esha's graduation, with presents and eating out at Esha's favorite restaurant. For Mohinder it was very good therapy. Esha took over most of the cooking responsibility of the family. Esha is a very good cook in general, especially with French dishes. Mohinder loved Esha's cooking.

Apparently Esha was quite popular with the staff at VOA and they were in contact with Esha quite regularly. They once asked Esha to come back and cover an event in New York City. Esha was interested to cover the event. Mohinder said, "Esha go and cover the event. It will be a good experience for you." Esha covered the event and her supervisor was so impressed with her performance that there was talk of a possible job offer.

Esha came back and gave us the good news. Mohinder stated, "Esha, I feel that you are going to be hired by VOA." We were so happy. In the meantime, we had a Mother's Day celebration with the whole family including three daughters and six of our grandchildren at the Biltmore Forest Country Club. After that, all of us were getting ready for Mohinder's 76th birthday. Sumandeep had a celebration at her home on May 12, Nina baked a cake and the family had a great party. Mohinder was very happy. On May 13, Mohinder's cousin, Nawal came from Vermont for the celebration. On May 14, Esha became in charge of the arrangement for her Nanima's birthday starting with flowers, presents and Mohinder's favorite breakfast. In the evening, there was a dinner in a downtown restaurant.

Mother's Day

Mohinder on her birthday

In June we were excited to celebrate our 56th wedding anniversary. On June 7, we shared our anniversary with flowers and a dinner in one of our favorite restaurants. Furthermore, we planned to spend some quality time together for which we reserved a room at the Pisgah Inn. The site is the peak of the Blue Ridge Parkway, a place to enjoy the sunrise and sunset over the Pisgah National Park Forest and mountains. Mohinder suggested, "We have an upstairs room to have a better view of the mountains." As the Pisgah Inn is a very popular place to stay during the summer months, the upstairs room was only available on June 21 at the earliest. We booked it and checked in on June 21. Our room had a balcony facing the Pisgah National Forest and Looking Glass Rock. We enjoyed the sunset from the balcony. Then we had dinner in Pisgah Inn restaurant, which is one of our favorite restaurants around Asheville. In the morning we watched the sunrise. It was a great sight as expected. Breakfast and lunch on the top of the mountain with such a beautiful view was also a special treat. It was short, however a very special time for us. Mohinder enjoyed walking around the Camping Ground Park close by and then suggested, "Let us go to the top of Pisgah Mountain." From the parking lot to the summit is about 700 ft. in height by a moderately rough and rocky hiking trail. The steps looked quite rough and steep. I said, "Are you sure." She smiled. We discarded the idea. Due to her treatment, Mohinder did not look strong enough to go up. As far as myself, I have a back problem. Her Chardi Kala attitude was inspirational. It was a wonderful wedding celebration, and an unforgettable experience.

At Anniversary dinner

At Pisgah Inn

Enjoying the mountain from Balcony

At Camp grounds

Bhen Ji and brother, Arvinderpal Singh, came to celebrate the 4th of July with us. Mohinder excitedly prepared the dinner with Bhen Ji's favorite dishes. We watched the fireworks, close to our home, from the front porch. We had an enjoyable time. Mohinder was keeping up with her favorite activities in and around the house. She enjoyed flowers in the front yard of the house. She loved to sit on the porch and appreciate the beautiful flowers and think about the Creator in its wonderful creation. According to Sikhism, the Creator lives in its creation.

Furthermore, she was keeping up with her cooking and enjoying the yard. We have an apple tree in our yard and it was loaded with ripe apples. She enjoyed picking apples and making apple pies and apple sauce, etc. She loved to share fruit and produce from the garden with our neighbors.

Mohinder's flowers in the front and apple tree

Mohinder was getting weaker due to the disease and treatment. We were regularly visiting her oncologist during the chemo therapy. The oncologist gave us the shocking news that the cancer had gone to her brain and for that Mohinder needed radiation treatment, and the chemo therapy should be stopped. When Nina got the news, she flew back from Bangkok. The Dr. said that chemo treatment would be resumed after the radiation treatment and hopefully the treatment would be successful. Mohinder was getting weaker and slowing down as the treatment was not working. At this point, Mohinder was worried about her family and still smiling, apparently she was ready to face the inevitable, the Will of God.

In the later part of May, Mohinder suggested to Bina to come and live at home. Bina agreed and moved back. She started helping Mohinder with the home work and enjoying mama's company. She quit her job. Mohinder was so happy about this. Mohinder asked me to take care of Bina. Quietly she was making sure that the family would be taken care of.

On the other hand, we assured her, "That you have done everything to make sure that we will be fine. We like to see you happy." She smiled and resumed her activities. On Aug.1, Mohinder asked me to have Sat SANG (prayer) up stair in Sri Guru Granth Sahib's room. We prepared Karhah Parshad and the whole family participated in the prayer. Although Mohinder was quite weak, however, she climbed the stairs and had her favorite Sabads (Gurbani hymns) sang which are:

1. Ham bheekhak bheekhaaree Thaarae thoo Nij Patt hai Dhaataa. (We are poor beggars of yours; you, Oh Lord, are the selfless Giver.)

2. Darasaan Dhaekh Jeevaan Gur Thaeraa. (Oh Lord, your vision in my mind is my life.)

3. Jaa Too Mayrai Val Hai Taa Kiaa Muhchhandaa. (When You are on my side, Lord, then I do not need any other help.)

4. Aukhee Gharee Na Dakhan Dayee Aapnaa Biradd Samaalay. (The Lord, because of His innate nature, does not let His devotee see any difficult time.)

5. Harr kaa Naam Radhai Nit Dhiaaeee. Thayraa keeaa Meettha Laagai. (Always meditate, in your mind, on the Name of the Lord − your Will Oh God is sweet to me.)

There was a recital from Sri Guru Granth Sahib Ji. It was an hour of prayer and recital. Karhah Parshad was distributed in a Sikh traditional way. Mohinder was very happy and contented.

A few days before the prayer, Mohinder asked Nina to send a message to Arvinderpal Singh that she would like to see him. Nina sent the message and Arvinderpal Singh came the next day. Mohinder was so happy to see him. They enjoyed the quality time being together.

Then Esha got the good news of the job offer from VOA and to start working first week of August, 2015. Seemingly, Esha was all set for her career. Mohinder was so excited and wanted to celebrate. We prepared a great dinner and a bottle of Champagne was opened to toast the occasion. It was a great feeling to see Mohinder so happy and smiling.

She wanted to see Esha settled in her career and happy. She was so thankful to God for all His blessings.

At Esha's job celebration dinner

On the evening of Aug 7, Mohinder was feeling weak. Nina and Bina slept with her. At around midnight Mohinder was feeling very uncomfortable. Bina and Nina felt the seriousness of the situation and called Sumandeep. Sumandeep and Mark came right away. Mohinder had one of her favorite disc of Gurbani Kirtan playing. The whole family, the five of us and Mark, were reciting repeatedly, "Sat Nam Sat Nam Sat Nam Ji, Waheguru Waheguru Waheguru Ji." Sumandeep, Nina and Mark were making Mohinder as comfortable as possible while I was holding her hand. At 1: 41 AM, Mohinder passed on to the heavenly abode with a sweet smile on her face.

According to Sikhism, this time is known as Amrit Wala, (ambrosial time) the best time for meditating on the name of God. It was also the celebration of Janam Dan, birthday, of our eighth Guru Sahib, Sri Guru Harkishan Sahib Ji. What a time and what a way to pass on! Mohinder prepared herself through her deeds and attitude during her life to be one with GOD. She was an exemplary Gur Sikh.

We informed the family members, relatives and friends about the sad news. Everyone was shocked as it was unexpected, and so sudden. By Saturday evening most of the family members and relatives arrived. Final services and saskar (cremation) were set for Sunday evening. Mohinder was so blessed that all arrangements were complete by Sunday noon. Although the closest Gurdwara Sahib with Bhai Ji (Sikh preacher) is in Charlotte NC, he came at very short notice to perform the services. Sikh tradition was followed with Mohinder's selected Sabads and traditional prayers.

After the services all guests came home and participated in the prayer with recital from Sri Guru Granth Sahib Ji. Services ended with the start of the complete recital, Sadharan Paath, of Sri Guru Granth Sahib Ji by the family members to accept the Will of God and endure the loss of Mohinder Ji. Sikh tradition was followed to offer the Astian (ashes) to a good flowing water. For that, Mark suggested a beautiful rapid river, the North Mills River, in the Pisgah National Forest only a few miles from Asheville. It was a lovely spot where the whole family participated in the offering. All went according to Mohinder's wishes and Sikh tradition. God takes care of His devotees. Mohinder was a firm believer in that.

Family at the North Mills River

She is survived by three wonderful daughters, seven grandchildren and lots of unforgettable memories and guidelines for us to follow her example to accept God's Will and live a successful and happy life.

Five of us

The whole family

In her life she touched the hearts of so many people and shared good will with them. She practiced and enjoyed a realistic Sikh way of living. Her guidance and wisdom during her life will always be a guiding light for us and generations to come. She used God's Gift of life the best possible way throughout her life, and she will always be with us through her memories.

www.ingramcontent.com/pod-product-compliance
Lightning Source LLC
LaVergne TN
LVHW010315070426
835510LV00024B/3390